Death and Grief

Healing through Group Support

Harold Ivan Smith

Augsburg Fortress, Minneapolis

Contents

INTERSECTIONS
Small Group Series

Death and Grief
Healing through Group Support

Developed in cooperation with the Division for Congregational Ministries

George S. Johnson, series introduction
Andrea Lee Schieber and William Congdon, editors
The Wells Group, series design
James L. Fly/Unicorn Stock Photos, cover photo

Copyright © 1995 Augsburg Fortress
All rights reserved. May not be reproduced.
ISBN 0-8066-0130-2
Printed on 50% recycled paper (10% postconsumer fibers)

5 6 7 8 9 0 1 2 3 4 5 6 7 8 9

Introduction

Fast relief?

In our hurry-up culture, we want fast answers, relief, and surefire fix-it solutions in a one, two, three format. We get the impression that we don't have time to grieve. In a culture that goes to great lengths to deny, to hide, even to camouflage death, millions of young adults do not have a firsthand acquaintance with mourning. Moreover, tomorrow's young adults—today's children—are often excluded from grief rituals.

Where can we find comfort?

Many of us know Jesus' words, "Blessed are those who mourn." Those last words, "for they will be comforted," are the ones we have difficulty with. Where can we find comfort? In a boutique at the mall or perhaps through a specialty mail-order catalog?

By now we have discovered that the rat-race called daily existence doesn't stop because of the loss we have experienced. We tip our hat politely at the rituals—because it is expected of us—and we're on our way: people to see, places to go, deadlines to meet. The only thing lacking in contemporary condolence cards is the unspoken inscription: Get over it! Life goes on.

The only problem is that life doesn't go on for some of us. An essential part of our lives has been extracted, perhaps violently, certainly without our cooperation. Now we have to answer the question: how do we navigate life without this one we grieve?

Our unique grief

We remember those little plastic signs hanging on the inside of the door of most motel or hotel rooms: Do not disturb. We hang that sign on our hearts. If you do the hard work of grieving in our society, you probably will do it alone.

Look at your fingerprints. No one in the world has prints exactly like yours. You are that unique. So it is with grief.

Choices

Anne Brener is right in saying, "The facts of [our] lives and the stories [we] have lived don't change. What can change is the way [we] feel about [our] history" (*Mourning & Mitzvah*, page 233). Nothing will change the essential reality of the death that has brought you to participate in this small group. But the six choices to be considered in this experience and ultimately either accepted or rejected, will determine the landscape of your grief.

The objectives of this small group experience are to help you:

- Recognize your loss
- React authentically, accurately, and adequately to your loss
- Recollect and reexperience your loss
- Relinquish the old attachments to the deceased
- Readjust adaptively to a new world
- Reach out to a new future

These can become first-person singular choices for you, choices you make.

Not just another group

This study is not designed to be "just another" support or self-help group. This is a healthy, safe place for you who are grieving to bring yourselves, your stories, your anger, your bewilderment, and to know that it's just likely that others will have been there and will recognize in your story parts of their story. And it is possible that something in your story will encourage another griever in this group.

"Blessed are those who mourn...."

SMALL GROUP SERIES

Welcome into the family of those who are part of small groups! Intersections Small Group Series will help you and other members of your group build relationships and discover ways to connect the Christian faith with your everyday life.

This book is prepared for those who want to make a difference in this world, who want to grow in their Christian faith, as well as for those who are beginning to explore the Christian faith. The information in this introduction to the Intersections small group experience can help your group make the most out of your time together.

Biblical encouragement

"Do not be conformed to this world, but be transformed by the renewing of your minds, so that you may discern what is the will of God—what is good and acceptable and perfect" *(Romans 12:2).*

Small groups provide an atmosphere where the Holy Spirit can transform lives. As you share your life stories and learn together, God's Spirit can work to enlighten and direct you.

Strength is provided to face the pressures to conform to forces and influences that are opposed to what is "good and acceptable and perfect." To "be transformed" is an ongoing experience of God's grace as we take up the cross and follow Jesus. Changed lives happen as we live in community with one another. Small groups encourage such change and growth.

What is a small group?

A number of definitions and descriptions of the small group ministry experience exist throughout the church. Roberta Hestenes, a Presbyterian pastor and author, defines a small group as an intentional face-to-face gathering of three to twelve people who meet regularly with the common purpose of discovering and growing in the possibilities of the abundant life.

Whatever definition you use, the following characteristics are important.

Small—Seven to ten people is ideal so that everyone can be heard and no one's voice is lost. More than twelve members makes genuine caring difficult.

Intentional—Commitment to the group is a high priority.

Personal—Sharing experiences and insights is more important than mastering content.

Conversational—Leaders that facilitate conversation, rather than teach, are the key to encouraging participation.

Friendly—Having a warm, accepting, nonjudgmental atmosphere is essential.

Christ-centered—The small group experience is biblically based, related to the real world, and founded on Christ.

Features of Intersections Small Group Series

A small group model

A number of small group ministry models exist. Most models include three types of small groups:

- *Discipleship groups*—where people gather to grow in Christian faith and life;

- *Support and recovery groups*—which focus on special interests, concerns, or needs; and

- *Ministry groups*—which have a task-oriented focus.

Intersections Small Group Series presently offers material for discipleship groups and support and recovery groups.

For discipleship groups, this series offers a variety of courses with Bible study at the center. What makes a discipleship group different from traditional group Bible studies? In discipleship groups, members bring their life experience to the exploration of the biblical material.

For support and recovery groups, Intersections Small Group Series offers topical material to assist group members in dealing with issues related to their common experience, hurt, or interest. An extra section of facilitator helps in the back of the book will assist leaders of support and recovery groups to anticipate and prepare for special circumstances and needs that may arise as group members explore a topic.

Ministry groups can benefit from an environment that includes prayer, biblical reflection, and relationship building, in addition to their task focus.

Four essentials

Prayer, personal sharing, biblical reflection, and a group ministry task are part of each time you gather. These are all important for Christian community to be experienced. Each of the six chapter themes in each book includes:

- Short prayers to open and close your time together.

- Carefully worded questions to make personal sharing safe, nonthreatening, and voluntary.

- A biblical base from which to understand and discover the power and grace of God. God's Word is the compass that keeps the group on course.

- A group ministry task to encourage both individuals and the group as a whole to find ways to put faith into action.

Flexibility

Each book contains six chapter themes that may be covered in six sessions or easily extended for groups that meet for a longer period of time. Each chapter theme is organized around two to three main topics with supplemental material to make it easily adaptable to your small group's needs. You need not use all the material. Most themes will work well for 1½- to 2-hour sessions, but a variety of scheduling options is possible.

Bible based

Each of the six chapter themes in the book includes one or more Bible texts printed in its entirety from the New Revised Standard Version of the Bible. This makes it easy for all group members to read and learn from the same text. Participants will be encouraged through questions, with exercises, and by other group members to address biblical texts in the context of their own lives.

User friendly

The material is prepared in such a way that it is easy to follow, practical, and does not require a professional to lead it. Designating one to be the facilitator to guide the group is important, but there is no requirement for this person to be theologically trained or an expert in the course topic. Many times options are given so that no one will feel forced into any set way of responding. The "Facilitator Helps" on pages 65-74 explain ways to adapt the material to the interests and needs of the group.

Group goals and process

1. **Creating a group covenant or contract for your time together will be important.** During your first meeting, discuss these important characteristics of all small groups and decide how your group will handle them.

Confidentiality—Agreeing that sensitive issues that are shared remain in the group.

Regular attendance—Agreeing to make meetings a top priority.

Nonjudgmental behavior—Agreeing to confess one's own shortcomings, if appropriate, not those of others, and not giving advice unless asked for it.

Prayer and support—Being sensitive to one another, listening, becoming a caring community.

Accountability—Being responsible to each other and open to change.

Items in your covenant should be agreed upon by all members. Add to the group covenant as you go along. Space to record key aspects is included in the back of this book. See page 76.

2. **Everyone is responsible for the success of the group, but do arrange to have one facilitator who can guide the group process each time you meet.**

The facilitator is not a teacher or healer. Teaching, learning, and healing happen from the group experience. The facilitator is more of a shepherd who leads the flock to where they can feed and drink and feel safe.

Remember, an important goal is to experience genuine love and community in a Christ-centered atmosphere. To help make this happen, the facilitator encourages active listening and honest sharing. This person allows the material to facilitate opportunities for self-awareness and interaction with others.

Leadership is shared in a healthy group, but the facilitator is the one designated to set the pace, keep the group focused, and enable the members to support and care for each other.

People need to sense trust and freedom as the group develops; therefore, avoid "shoulds" or "musts" in your group.

3. **Taking on a group ministry task can help members of your group balance personal growth with service to others.**

In your first session, identify ways your group can offer help to others within the church or in your surrounding community. Take time at each meeting to do or arrange for that ministry task. Many times it is in the doing that we discover what we believe or how God is working in our lives.

4. **Starting or continuing a personal action plan offers a way to address personal needs that you become aware of in your small group experience.**

For example, you might want to spend more time in conversation with a friend or spouse. Your action plan might state, "I plan to visit with Terry two times before our next small group meeting."

If you decide to pursue a personal action plan, consider sharing it with your small group. Your group can be helpful in at least three ways: by giving support; helping to define the plan in realistic, measurable ways; and offering a source to whom you can be accountable.

5. **Prayer is part of small group fellowship.** There is great power in group prayer, but not everyone feels free to offer spontaneous prayer. That's okay.

Learning to pray aloud takes time and practice. If you feel uncomfortable, start with simple and short prayers. And remember to pray for other members between sessions.

Use page 77 in the back of this book to note prayer requests made by group members.

6. **Consider using a journal to help reflect on your experiences and insights between meeting times.**

Writing about feelings, ideas, and questions can be one way to express yourself; plus it helps you remember what so often gets lost with time.

The "Daily Walk" component includes material that can get your journaling started. This, of course, is up to you and need not be done on any regular schedule. Even doing it once a week can be time well spent.

How to use this book

The material provided for each session is organized around some key components. If you are the facilitator for your small group, be sure to read this section carefully.

NOTE: Those who plan (or might plan) to lead this small group should read the "Facilitator Helps" starting on page 65.

The facilitator's role is to establish a hospitable atmosphere and set a tone that encourages participants to share, reflect, and listen to each other. Some important practical things can help make this happen.

- Whenever possible meet in homes. Be sure to provide clear directions about how to get there.

- Use name tags for several sessions.

- Place the chairs in a circle and close enough for everyone to hear and feel connected.

- Be sure everyone has access to a book; preparation will pay off.

Welcoming

The meeting room should be self-contained so that participants can speak without fear of being overheard. Arrange the furniture so that everyone can see each other.

If you wish to add pictures or visuals to the room, choose ones that show new life or hope arising out of despair, such as pictures of seedlings, dawn, rainbows, or Christian symbols of life and death. Ask for ideas from the group members for making the room a welcoming place.

A table with coffee, tea, juice, and cookies could be set up near the room's entrance. If you want to have refreshments for each session, determine at the first meeting if they will be supplied on a rotating basis and who is willing to help with this task.

Focus

Each of the six chapter themes in this book has a brief focus statement. Read it aloud. It will give everyone a sense of the direction for each session and provide some boundaries so that people will not feel lost or frustrated trying to cover everything. The focus also connects the theme to the course topic.

Community building

This opening activity is crucial to a relaxed, friendly atmosphere. It will prepare the ground for gradual group development. Two "Community Building" options are provided under each theme. With the facilitator giving his or her response to the questions first, others are free to follow.

One purpose for this section is to allow everyone to participate as he or she responds to nonthreatening questions. The activity serves as a check-in time when participants are invited to share how things are going or what is new.

Make this time light and fun; remember, humor is a welcome gift. Use fifteen to twenty minutes for this activity in your first few sessions and keep the entire group together.

During your first meeting, encourage group members to write down names and phone numbers (when appropriate) of the other members, so people can keep in touch. Use page 75 for this purpose.

Discovery

This component focuses on exploring the theme for your time together, using material that is read, and questions and exercises that encourage sharing of personal insights and experiences.

Reading material includes a Bible text with commentary written by the topic writer. Have volunteers read the Bible texts aloud. Read the commentary aloud only when it seems helpful. The main passage to be used is printed so that everyone operates from a common translation and sees the text.

"A Further Look" is included in some places to give you additional study material if time permits. Use it to explore related passages and questions. Be sure to have your own Bible handy.

Questions and exercises related to the theme will invite personal sharing and storytelling. Keep in mind that as you listen to each other's stories, you are inspired to live more fully in the grace and will of God. Such exchanges make Christianity relevant and transformation more likely to happen. Caring relationships are key to clarifying one's beliefs. Sharing personal experiences and insights is what makes the small group spiritually satisfying.

Most people are open to sharing their life stories, especially if they're given permission to do so and they know someone will actively listen. Starting with the facilitator's response usually works best. On some occasions you may want to break the group into units of three or four persons to explore certain questions. When you reconvene, relate your experience to the whole group. The phrase "Explore and Relate," which appears occasionally in the margin, refers to this recommendation. Encourage couples to separate for this smaller group activity. Appoint someone to start the discussion.

Wrap-up

Plan your schedule so that there will be enough time for wrapping up. This time can include work on your group ministry task, review of key discoveries during your time together, identifying personal and prayer concerns, closing prayers, and the Lord's Prayer.

The facilitator can help the group identify and plan its ministry task. Introduce the idea and decide on your group ministry task during "Wrap-up" time in the first session. Tasks need not be grandiose. Activities might include:

- Ministry in your community, such as "adopting" a food shelf, clothes closet, or homeless shelter; sponsoring equipment, food, or clothing drives; or sending members to staff the shelter.

- Ministry to members of the church, such as writing notes to those who are ill or bereaved.

- Church tasks where volunteers are always needed, such as serving refreshments during the fellowship time after worship, stuffing envelopes for a mailing, or taking responsibility for altar preparations for one month.

Depending upon the task, you can use part of each meeting time to carry out or plan the task.

In the "Wrap-up," allow time for people to share insights and encouragements and to voice special prayer requests. Just to mention someone who needs prayer is a form of prayer. The "Wrap-up" time may include a brief worship experience with candles, prayers, and singing. You might form a circle and hold hands. Silence can be effective. If you use the Lord's Prayer in your group, select the version that is known in your setting. There is space on page 77 to record the version your group uses. Another closing prayer is also printed on page 77. Before you go, ask members to pray for one another during the week. Remember also any special concerns or prayer requests.

Daily walk

Seven Bible readings and a thought, prayer, and verse for the journey related to the material just discussed are provided for those who want to keep the theme before them between sessions. These brief readings may be used for devotional time. Some group members may want to memorize selected passages. The Bible readings can also be used for supplemental study by the group if needed. Prayer for other group members can also be part of this time of personal reflection.

A word of encouragement

No material is ever complete or perfect for every situation or group. Creativity and imagination will be important gifts for the facilitator to bring to each theme. Keep in mind that it is in community that we are challenged to grow in Jesus Christ. Together we become what we could not become alone. It is God's plan that it be so.

For additional resources and ideas see *Starting Small Groups—and Keeping Them Going* (Minneapolis: Augsburg Fortress, 1995).

1 Recognizing Your Loss

The first healthy choice toward healing after a significant death is to fully recognize that loss.

Community building

Option

Share a time from your childhood when you confronted or failed to confront fear. Have you ever discovered that an experience you feared was not what you had anticipated? Share such experiences with each other.

What is your biggest fear in participating in a small group?

What was the scariest part about coming to this group?

This small group will provide you a safe place to admit, face, and embrace your loss. To help you to get to know each other and to learn about each other's grief, take turns giving responses to as many of the four statements listed below as you choose. First state your name.

- My loss was (name), my (relationship).
- (Name) died (how),_____ (when)_____.
- If I had to summarize my grief experience in one word, that word would be _____.
- So far, from this loss, I have learned _____.

Opening prayer

God, from you no thoughts, secrets, moods, or losses are hidden. Give us the courage to fully recognize our loss(es) and to share our loss with you and with this group. Amen.

Goal setting

For a description of goal setting, see page 7.

Why participate in a grief group? Many who need such a group would never participate in one! People will ask you, "What is that group all about?" How would you answer them? We all come with different expectations about what this group will do for us.

Read through this list of possible goals for your group. Then rank the goals in the space provided according to your preferences, from 1 (most important goal) to 11 (least important goal). Perhaps you want to add a goal of your own to the list. Use the blank space for that.

Write down the goals the group chooses on page 76 in the Appendix.

After a few moments, you will have an opportunity to share your list with the entire group.

Potential goals for this group

_____ To help group members experience an atmosphere of trust, honesty, and openness.

_____ To help group members find a sense of hope.

_____ To help group members heal.

_____ To help group members identify and understand problems, issues, and feelings emerging from the death.

_____ To help group members understand that others have experienced similar problems and feelings after loss.

_____ To help group members identify and remove emotional, psychological, and spiritual barriers to a relationship with God that has been affected by death.

_____ To help group members assume responsibility for their futures.

_____ To help group members in their recovery.

_____ To help group members identify unfinished business which affects them in the present and which will affect them in the future.

_____ To relieve the load on pastor and counselors.

_____ To provide group members a safe place to grieve.

_____ Other:_____.

Traditions of public mourning

Read and discuss as a group.

The black armband has become a relic in our culture. In the past, however, following a significant death, individuals tied a black cloth around their upper arms as a public symbol that they had been recently touched by a death.

In pictures taken early in World War II, one sees an armband on President Franklin Roosevelt's sleeve; his mother had died in September 1941. During the war, the presence of a gold star in a residential window announced the death of a family member in the war.

Those growing up in the fifties and sixties may remember seeing floral bouquets attached to the front doors of houses or businesses after a family member's death. The flowers were reminding signals that notified even strangers of a death.

Historically, widows were expected to wear black, perhaps for as long as a year, and to turn down social invitations.

Though now archaic, these traditions were helpful reminders to grieving individuals, and to those with whom they came in contact, of the presence of active, community-sanctioned mourning.

- How does your community symbolize loss following a death?
- Is your community healthier for having fewer public grief symbols?
- What, from your experience, would be a helpful public grief symbol or tradition?

A proverb says that although everyone knows that death happens, no one wants to believe it. Let's look at some realities that help us recognize our loss through death.

Task 1: Recognize that some people do not understand

Read and discuss.

Many people have difficulty understanding the specific nuances of your loss. People say, "I know what you are going through" to suggest "I recognize your loss and grief." But they may appreciate only the surface loss. Their words may seem like just a cliché.

- What are some clichés you have been offered?
- What would it take for someone to really be able to say, "I know what you are going through"?
- Have you ever said (or wanted to say), "You have no idea what I am going through!"?

One psalmist experienced a shortage of helpers and prayed, "Do not be far from me, for trouble is near and there is no one to help me" (Psalm 22:11).

With dysfunctional families and relationships a reality for millions, you may not find many who fully appreciate your loss. You may have been stunned or hurt by a callous, "What? Still grieving? Maybe you need to see a shrink," or the more polite, "Get some professional help."

- Has anyone questioned the way you are grieving?
- What did they say or imply?
- Circle the best verb: You may have been annoyed, disappointed, angered, or _____ by friends and family members who only politely acknowledged and recognized your loss.

We live in a replaceable society; to some, death is just another opportunity for replacement. Some may even distance themselves from you as long as you are grieving. Your grief reminds them, "This could happen to me!" or triggers unfinished grief business within them.

If you are younger, your friends may have not had significant deaths in their lives—yet. So, they may be at a real loss to fully recognize and respond to your grief.

- Who has "distanced" themselves from you and your grief?

Others have filters through which they offer condolences. Suppose your elderly mother dies. Sally, your longtime friend who has a mother lingering with Alzheimer's disease, attempting to comfort you, may say, "You should (two dangerous words to anyone who is grieving) be glad that she went quickly." Another friend may say, "You should not be sad. She lived a long life." Such statements discount your loss.

■ What have you been told to do or not do with your grief?

What are intended to be comforting words can sting, irritate, and lacerate. Days later you may find yourself fuming, "I can't believe she or he said that to me!" One grief complication is that grievers continually "relisten" to advice, as if it were a cassette or videotape.

■ How have you handled insensitive comments? Check all that apply:

____ Ignored them   ____ Walked away

____ Confronted the speaker   ____ Talked to a third party

____ Pretended I didn't hear   ____ Inwardly fumed

____ Can members of the group suggest other ways?

■ Have any of you had a family member or friend overwhelmed by your loss?

■ What family member or friend most fully recognizes your loss? What has made that individual so sensitive to your loss? Go around the group to answer these two questions with a) the person's name, b) your relationship to that person, and c) what has made that person so sensitive.

■ How have friends, neighbors, colleagues, or family members officially or socially recognized your loss? In the spaces below, write **MH** for the most helpful ways and **LH** for the least helpful ways.

_____ Cards

_____ Personal visits

_____ Phone calls

_____ Flowers

_____ Donation to a designated charity

_____ Food

_____ Dropping by

_____ Prayer

_____ Remembered anniversary of the death

_____ "Come along with us" invitations

_____ Pastoral visits

_____ Sent "I am thinking of you" notes weeks/ months after the death

_____ Recognizes "tough" days or occasions

_____ Other

A further look

■ Go back and reread Sally's words on page 14. How would you reply to her? Have one group member read Sally's comments; have another group member creatively respond. Then have the group discuss the improvisation.

Discovery

Task 2: Recognize the impact of a loss

Explore and relate. **Explore in groups of three or four; then relate a brief summary to the entire group.**

Did you play "let's pretend" games as a child? Many grievers play "let's pretend this death has not happened." Even the words in reporting a death are often softened. Instead of saying that a person died, we say (fill in the blanks):

This person _____.

Some people immediately and thoroughly remove any reminders of a relationship. On February 13, 1884, young Theodore Roosevelt was passing out cigars on the floor of the New York Assembly and accepting congratulations on the birth of his daughter, Alice. Within hours, that joy was shattered by a telegram informing him that his wife and mother were both dying.

It took five long hours for Roosevelt to reach his home; he rushed to his wife's side and held her for hours. Some time after 2:00 A.M. came the message that if he wanted to say good-bye to his mother, he had to come now. He walked down one flight of stairs to her bedroom and watched her die. Then he returned to his wife's side.

About 2:00 P.M. on Valentine's Day, the second Mrs. Roosevelt died. That night, the future president slashed a large cross across his diary and scrawled, "The light has gone out in my life."

After the funeral, one biographer commented, "Roosevelt set about dislodging his wife Alice Lee, from his soul." Other than two brief valedictories, "there is no record of Roosevelt ever mentioning her name again," even to the daughter named for her. Even his *Autobiography*, written years later, made no mention of Alice Lee. After his death in 1919, aides destroyed almost everything in his extensive correspondence and memorabilia linking Teddy and Alice (see Edward Morris, *The Rise of Theodore Roosevelt*, pages 240-245).

- What annoys you in reading this?

- What surprises you?

- What do you think motivated Roosevelt to go to such lengths to "dislodge" Alice from his memory?

- What actions have you taken to "dislodge" the person you have lost?

  ____ Gave away clothes

  ____ Put away photos

  ____ Gave away possessions

  ____ Moved

  ____ Put personal items in storage

  ____ Changed churches

  ____ Other actions: _____

- Have you made any premature dislodging choices that you now regret?

Discovery

Task 3: Recognize God's active concern for you

Read and discuss.

For some, the most difficult grieving task is to realize that God cares. Indeed, many thoughts about God only compound our grief. Some snarl, "God could have prevented this! Why didn't God heal _____(name)? Why didn't God prevent _____ (name)'s death?" We don't know.

- When I hear or read that God is concerned about me,

  I feel _____

  I think _____

  I wonder _____

  I would like to ask God _____

"Why?" is probably the most common grief-linked question. Millions have wrestled with it. Even if we knew the answer, we would still ask the question.

One reason for Jesus' coming to earth was to help us with our why questions. He came to live among us, to help us understand that he understands us. John's Gospel contains an incredible account of Jesus fully experiencing the death of his friend Lazarus.

John 11:17, 21-26, 32-35, 38a

Read aloud.

**17When Jesus arrived, he found that Lazarus had already been in the tomb four days.... 21Martha said to Jesus, "Lord, if you had been here, my brother would not have died. 22But even now I know that God will give you whatever you ask of him." 23Jesus said to her, "Your brother will rise again." 24Martha said to him, "I know that he will rise again in the resurrection on the last day." 25Jesus said to her, "I am the resurrection and the life. Those who believe in me, even though they die, will live, 26and everyone who lives and believes in me will never die...."
32When Mary came where Jesus was and saw him, she knelt at his feet and said to him, "Lord, if you had been here, my brother would not have died." 33When Jesus saw her weeping, ...he was greatly disturbed in spirit and deeply moved. 34He said, "Where have you laid him?" They said to him, "Lord, come and see." 35Jesus began to weep. 38Then Jesus, again greatly disturbed, came to the tomb.**

Slowly reread this passage. Circle the key words or phrases that grab your attention.

■ What surprises you in this account?

■ What seems inconsiderate?

You may find it difficult to translate the Lazarus story into your loss. Or you may identify with Martha's anger or with the grumblers who asked questions. But the reality remains, then and now: Jesus deeply cares. Isaiah 53:3, a verse often used to describe Jesus, calls the servant of God "a man of sorrows, and familiar with suffering" (NIV).

Healthy bereavement begins when a grieving person says: "This *is* happening and this is happening to *me*." Healthy grief begins when I say "(name), my (relationship), died." Blessed are those who fully recognize their loss(es).

■ How have you recognized your grief? Name three ways.

Wrap-up

See page 10 in the introduction for a description of "Wrap-up."

Before you go, take time for the following:

- Group ministry task

- Review

- Personal concerns and prayer concerns

- Closing prayers

Daily walk

Bible readings

Day 1
Psalm 137:1-6

Day 2
Psalm 138:3, 7-8

Day 3
Isaiah 53:2-5

Day 4
Psalm 27:4-7

Day 5
Psalm 28:6-7

Day 6
Ecclesiastes 3:1-8

Day 7
Lamentations 3:22-24

Thought for the journey

As you look for the fingerprints of God in your life in this loss, think about where they would be. Has God worked through a kind friend? A caring pastor or church? Have you overlooked God's care?

Prayer for the journey

Friend of grievers, you are acquainted with sorrows and griefs. You are touched by the feelings of our losses. Be with us on our grief journey. Give us the courage to fully recognize our losses and bring them to you. Amen.

Verse for the journey

"For he did not despise or abhor the affliction of the afflicted; he did not hide his face from me, but heard me when I cried to him" (Psalm 22:24).

2 Reacting to Your Loss

The second healthy choice toward healing after a significant death is to react, feel, and experience the loss authentically, accurately, and adequately.

Community building

Option

Loss is a basic element in living. Share a memory of some object, pet, or person that you lost in childhood. What did you learn from that loss?

If you prefer, share a moment when you thought you had lost something but then found it.

Think about this statement: "My son's death was the greatest disappointment and disaster in my life, the one I have never been able to forget completely."

- Share with the group your greatest disappointment and/or disaster.

- Take turns responding to this statement: "If I were to share with _____ (name, relationship) what I am feeling about this loss, she/he would (do or say) _____."

Opening prayer

Sustainer, you have richly endowed us with a wide range of emotions from which to respond to the crises, surprises, outrages, and joys of life. Give us insight into our reaction and response skills. Amen.

Read aloud.

Have you ever ridden the high-speed underground trams that link the terminals in airports like the one in Atlanta? Recently, I boarded a tram that was being taken out of service. "Slow" didn't do it justice. As the tram slowly crawled down the dark tunnel (I missed my plane), I thought, "This is like grief." Some grievers whiz through the dark tunnel of loss; others plod foot by foot. In previous losses, you may have experienced a different "speed" of grief, and that may make this most recent death even more confusing. Still, to reach the destination of healing—*reconciliation* rather than *recovery* or *resolution*—we must choose to react authentically, accurately, and adequately.

Task 1: To authentically grieve and mourn

Read aloud and discuss.

What is your grief style? If we have a lifestyle, it is only natural that we also have a "grief style."

Perhaps we should formally define two key words that are often used interchangeably. They are *grieve* and *mourn*.

- Take a moment with another group member to define *grieve* and *mourn* between the two of you. When all have finished, share your working definition with the group.

- Now read the definitions framed by Dr. Alan Wolfelt, Director of the Center for Loss and Life Transition:

   "*Grief* is the thoughts and feelings that are experienced within oneself upon the death of someone loved."

   "*Mourning* is taking the internal experience of grief and expressing it outside of oneself."

   Alan D. Wolfelt, "Dispelling 5 Common Myths About Grief," page 26.

- If you had to condense Dr. Wolfelt's definition of *grief* into one word, what would it be?

- Try to capture the meaning of *mourning* in a single word.

Perhaps you said that grief is internal while mourning is external. Wolfelt contends that some people grieve longer than necessary because they have never been allowed—let alone encouraged—to mourn, especially in a death-denying, increasingly rithalless culture.

Discuss as a group.

Consider this

Wolfelt suggests that mourning is "grief gone public" ("Dispelling 5 Common Myths About Grief," page 26). But how can one authentically mourn in a culture that prefers the experience to be privatized and kept out of sight?

Read aloud and discuss.

Have you ever heard the expression, "Live and let live"? Well, let's modify that to say, "Grieve and let grieve"! Each of us must grieve in our own way and on our own timetable, but we must also have a safe environment—such as family, friends, neighbor or church—in which to invest authentically in that grief work.

It is amazing what people say to each other at funeral homes and cemeteries. "How is John?" someone asks. "Oh," an observer responds with a hint of admiration, "he's holding up very well!" which translates, "Attaboy!" Or we may ask, "How's Mary taking this?" and hear, "She's being so strong!"

So many of us are afraid of "going to pieces" that we douse or disown our God-given emotions. But "going to pieces" could actually be physically, emotionally, and spiritually authentic and healthy. Wolfelt suggests that those who are "self-permitting" with their emotions grieve in healthier ways and for shorter periods of time.

Blockages to authentic grief

Explore and relate.

Let's look at who and what can block your authentic expression of grief:

Families can be "closed" communicators when they do not let any outsiders in or risk being vulnerable. When asked how they are, they say, "Very well, under the circumstances." Three common rules are: Don't talk! Don't trust! Don't feel!

Male peers may try to block our grief. Because of the machismo in our society, we believe that men are supposed to be able to "take it" impassively. Consequently, some men drink out their grief, while others struggle to keep from crying, as did Robert Dole during his eulogy for the late Richard Nixon.

The church and its members sometimes misinterpret 1 Thessalonians 4:13, which reads "... so that you may not grieve as others do who have no hope." They read the verse as a condemnation of grieving: "don't grieve." Other believers may even intimidate or shame the griever with statements like "She is with the Lord" that imply "So why are you grieving?"

A vague notion of something called "stages" can get in the way. While the theory of five stages of grief is deeply ingrained in our culture, the originator, Elisabeth Kübler-Ross, never intended that her ideas be carved into stone. To declare that the stages must be set, predictable, ordered, and unfailingly sequential (like baseball's first, second, and third bases) harms grievers and blocks their authentic expression of grief.

Comparison to other grievers does not help us. The answer to your "How long?" is, "As long as it takes." We are devoted to techniques and to short cuts. We ask, "Am I doing my grief right?" or "Am I doing it like (name)? "One spouse may say to the other, "Come on. I'm over it. So should you!"

In order to authentically grieve, sometimes we have to ignore the impatience of the shaming person. "Aren't you over this *yet?*" wounds us even when it comes from those who claim to love us the most.

- Who (if anyone) has attempted to interfere with or interrupt your authentic grief?

- In the margin, write the names of persons to whom you compare your own grief style.

Read and discuss .

Consider this

[1]"How long, O Lord? Will you forget me forever? How long will you hide your face from me?

[2]How long must I bear pain in my soul, and have sorrow in my heart all day long? How long shall my enemy be exalted over me?" (Psalm 13:1-2)

- Examine another translation of this psalm of lament for insight. Copy the other translation in the margin.

Read and discuss as a
group.

Task 2: To appropriately grieve and mourn

One imposing barrier to healing is that our grieving must be
done in a culture that does not mourn well, and from which
death rituals are rapidly disappearing. Once upon a time, people died at home rather than in nursing homes, hospices, or
hospitals; people died in the presence of kin and friends. The
Bible speaks about Abraham's death: "This is the length of
Abraham's life, one hundred seventy-five years. Abraham
breathed his last and died in a good old age... and was gathered to his people. His sons Isaac and Ishmael buried him in
the cave of Machpelah... with his wife Sarah" (Genesis 25:7-
11).

- What in this account attracts your attention? Who buried
  Abraham? What is unusual or extraordinary about this?
  It's fascinating because earlier, Ishmael had been driven
  away into the desert by Abraham so that he could not
  compete with the favored heir, Isaac. Now, at their father's grave, the brothers or competitors meet again.

- Do you respond favorably or unfavorably to the phrase,
  "and was gathered to his people"? What mental images
  do you have when you hear or read this phrase? A family reunion? Deathbeds, historically, have not been off-
  limits. In fact, people hoped for a "good death"—
  meaning dying in their own bed—with time to mend relationships, to honor friendships, and to pass on bless-
  ings as well as to say good-bye.

Our culture once demanded a visitation, initially in the residence of the deceased. As people moved to cities and had
smaller homes, mortuaries became funeral *homes*. Visitation
with the family to pay one's respect as well as viewing the
body were expected; small children were never excluded. No
one thought a child would be harmed by exposure to the realities of life and death.

After visitation came the funeral. In many communities you
attended the funeral even if you did not know the person who
had died, as a way of showing respect. Cars stopped on the
street as the funeral procession passed.

Share with the group some funeral rituals of the past that you
have experienced.

- Were there any rituals that you feel harmed you?

- Were there any rituals that helped you?

Today, we're busy, and death is admittedly inconvenient. We're in something of a cultural rush to get it over. Ritual is increasingly minimized, especially for older people. We are too busy to grieve. Let a major world leader die and listen to the howl of protest if the televised rituals interfere with the soaps, game shows, or talk shows.

Private disposal is becoming a new trend. No funeral or memorial services, just speedy cremation. No mourning. If you must grieve, do us a favor, and do it in private. Memorial Day is merely a time to barbecue or go to the lake; the day officially launches summer.

Discovery

Task 3: To adequately grieve and mourn

Refer back to Wolfelt's definitions on page 21.

A person can authentically and appropriately grieve yet not be able to adequately mourn. Mental health professionals are increasingly aware of the hidden grievers and disenfranchised or unrecognized griefs.

Read and discuss.

When Nina's longtime friend and neighbor died, the estranged family swept into town and purged her condo overnight. After selecting what they wanted, they dumped the rest into large plastic bags. From her window, Nina watched—through salty tears—the pile of bags grow beside the dumpster. "I wish I could have had something of hers to keep, like a cup and saucer." No one recognized Nina's loss. After all, she wasn't family, *just* a friend. This level of grief goes unrecognized and therefore unsupported in a family-oriented culture.

Some cannot adequately grieve because a spouse discourages them. "I hate," one man snarled, "walking into that house and feeling like I'm back at the funeral home! She drags me down!" As a result, his wife grieves alone.

Some have to create what Jewish people called *mehom hanekhama*, "a place of comfort." It could be in your church, or a park, or even a room in your home, where you can go and do grief work without being interrupted, interrogated, or shamed.

Wolfelt has identified five categories of people who try to avoid grief: postponers, displacers, replacers, minimizers, and somaticizers.

Postponers believe, not unlike unwanted telephone callers, that if you put grief on hold it will eventually go away. For example, some who become single parents of young children declare, "I cannot deal with this now, I have children to think about. Maybe later."

■ Have you postponed any element of your grief?

Displacers mothball their grief but transfer their distress to other relationships. Displacers try to stay so busy with other emotions and activities that they have neither time nor energy for active grieving.

■ How might you have displaced your grief?

Replacers, rather than deal with the grief issues, take their emotions and invest them prematurely in new or transitional relationships. Observers are confused and assume that the griever must not have loved the deceased if he or she so quickly initiates a new relationship. Men with children are generally the record-setters for rapid remarriage.

■ Think of some expressions we use when a person initiates premature relationships.

Minimizers acknowledge the loss but dilute its impact. We assume that people have already done their grieving if the deceased dies after a long illness. Not necessarily. Many minimizers are motivated by religious influences. "Oh, she's with the Lord," or "He's out of his suffering." Minimizing is a common response to the death of a friend or even a pet. "He was just a friend" or "a dog, for heaven's sake!" We minimize an older adult's death by saying, "She lived a long life." The death of a child evokes a great deal of minimizing. One young couple was told, "Oh, you're young! You'll have another child," and what went unspoken was, "to replace this one."

Some minimizers try to rank griefs. Some, for example, insist that the death of a child is the greatest loss. Your grief, quite candidly, is just not as emotionally intense or deserving of recognition. Indeed, even in some grief groups, some members subtly minimize another group member's grief.

■ What are some minimizing phrases you've heard, or even used?

Somaticizers are individuals who avoid dealing with the grief directly, and instead develop symptoms of sickness so that the body can get the nongriever's attention. Wolfelt contends that some people unconsciously adopt this role in order to get emotional needs met. Somaticizers "fear that if they were to express their true feelings or grief [adequately grieve] that people would pull away and leave them feeling abandoned"

Adapted from *Death and Grief: A Guide for Clergy* by Alan Wolfelt, copyright © 1988 Accelerated Development, Inc. Reprinted by permission of Taylor and Francis.

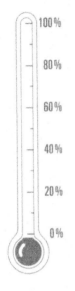

■ Which of these designations has been or is a currently accurate description of your grief style? Go around the group and say, "My name is _____ and I am a _____" (pick one of Wolfelt's categories). Of course, some of you might feel that your grief style resembles more than one of the categories.

How long does it take to adequately grieve a death? Only you can answer that. A healthy suggestion: Give yourself plenty of time. Grief and mourning may well be a marathon, not a sprint.

■ Think about those oversized thermometers used for fundraising campaigns to show what percentage of the goal has been reached. In the thermometer in the margin, color in the percentage of resolution of grief that you think you have reached.

Read and discuss.

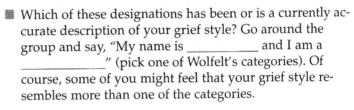

Consider this

Anne Brener states, "Few people ever feel completely finished with mourning... but our status as mourner does change" (*Mourning & Mitzvah*, pages 209-207). Brener offers two wonderful word pictures to symbolize this moment of recognition that it is time to move on: "to put a border around our grief work" (page 206) and "to put a fence around these feelings and move on" (page 221).

■ Can you think of a word or phrase that captures the decision to move on?

Abraham had many stories from the years he had spent with
Sarah. When she died at age 127—after more than a century of
marriage—Abraham struggled with the loss: "Sarah lived one
hundred twenty-seven years; this was the length of Sarah's
life. And Sarah died at Kiriath-arba (that is Hebron) in the
land of Canaan; and Abraham went in to mourn for Sarah and
to weep over her. Abraham rose up from beside his dead wife"
(Genesis 23:1-3a).

Abraham no doubt mourned authentically, appropriately, and
adequately. Look at the fascinating observation: "Abraham
rose up from beside his dead." Rose up. It does not say, although he too was elderly, that "he was lifted up." "Rose up"
sounds much more active. The patriarch went on with life—
only without Sarah.

- Can or will this be said of you? "(Your name) rose up
  from beside his or her dead."

- Circle the most appropriate answers to the following
  questions:

  a. Have you grieved authentically?
     Yes   No   Uncertain

  b. Have you grieved appropriately?
     Yes   No   Uncertain

  c. Have you grieved adequately?
     Yes   No   Uncertain

- What decisions or choices did you (or would you have
  to) make in order to answer yes to those questions? Remember, you always have some element of decision.

Consider this

In Columbia, South Carolina, there is a fascinating epitaph
on the grave of a young father who died of cancer. The first
two sentences have continued to haunt me:

**I DO NOT CHOOSE TO BE A COMMON MAN!
IT IS MY RIGHT TO BE UNCOMMON. . .**

The grave is that of the late Lee Atwater, former chairman
of the Republican National Committee and a powerful influence in Washington politics.

If you take time to authentically, appropriately, and adequately
grieve, you will be uncommon in this death-denying culture.
However, you will be emotionally and spiritually healthier for
that choice.

Wrap-up

See page 10 in the introduction for a description of "Wrap-up" items. See page 77 for a suggested closing prayer.

Before you go, take time for the following:

- **Group ministry task**

- **Review**

- **Personal concerns and prayer concerns**

- **Closing prayers**

Daily walk

Bible readings

Day 1
Jeremiah 31:10-13

Day 2
2 Samuel 12:15b-25

Day 3
Genesis 24:56-67

Day 4
Mark 16:1-11

Day 5
Luke 7:11-17

Day 6
Isaiah 61:1-4

Day 7
Romans 8:14-19, 35-39

Thought for the journey

Blessed are those who authentically, appropriately, and adequately grieve, for they will be healed and will model a healthier grief style to others.

Prayer for the journey

God, it hurts to feel and to fully experience this loss. It is tempting to short-circuit this grief; to just want to get it over with! Give us the courage you gave so that we too may "rise up from our dead" and walk into the future with you. Amen.

Verse for the journey

"Then you shall call, and the Lord will answer; you shall cry for help, and he will say, 'Here I am'" (Isaiah 58:9a).

3 Recollecting and Reexperiencing

The third choice toward healing after a significant death is to recollect and reexperience that loss.

Community building

Option

Pass around pictures from magazines. Study a photo, then relate it to your grief experience. If nothing comes to mind, say "pass" and hand it on. Some of us are particularly affected by commercials at certain holidays or milestones. Share with the group the gist of a commercial that can do a sneak attack on your emotions.

Many people collect things: china, stamps, quilts, coins, antiques, whatever. The dictionary says that to collect is to gather or to bring together to one place. This small group is a collection of griefs and losses. But it is also a collection of hope and experience based upon what you have learned as active grievers.

Some of the following questions are repeated from the previous session but they are helpful for remembering. Give only the information you wish to disclose.

- My first name is _____.
- My loss was (Name) who was my (relationship).
- (Name) died (when).
- I collect _____ and have for (how long). The reason I collect _____ is_____.
- How did the deceased influence what you collect?

Opening prayer

Divine Rememberer, you know us and you know our emotional framework. You know that in our grief we feel fragile, vulnerable. Help us to realistically, redemptively, and responsively remember those who have died. Amen.

Read and discuss as a group.

Have you ever heard the phrase, "Maybe *this* will refresh your memory?" Most grieving people have no difficulty remembering, but they struggle with prioritizing memories: What should I remember and what should I forget? Bob Hope's theme song for his television specials was "Thanks for the Memories." Many grieving persons can hum that along with Bob. We are thankful for the memories of good times or of better times.

- If you wish, share with the group a memory tied to the person who has died for which you can honestly say, "Thanks." Some cannot easily or honestly say that; some of you may feel uneasy or "put on the spot." Not all of us have those "precious memories" that country singers sing about.

- Maybe you can think of an image or analogy for your struggle with memories, such as "Memory is like roses in winter, or smiles with tears." Take a moment to think before answering.

Memory is like _____.

Memory is like _____.

Memory is like _____.

Task 1: Review the relationship realistically

Read and discuss.

"Speak no ill of the dead" is a injunction that many people take to heart.

- Have you known anyone to go overboard in this regard?

- What are some expressions that discourage negative but nonetheless realistic statements about the dead?

Families and friends may collaborate to create a fictional reality or a facade—not unlike a Hollywood movie set—about the deceased. Families have secrets they keep from the outside world and sometimes from particular family members, as in the case of an affair or spousal abuse or incest; such realities hamstring the ability to grieve. Or, some details of the cause or circumstances of the death may be edited or withheld to protect the deceased or the family reputation. This can happen in the case of suicide, or of AIDS where outsiders believe the death was cancer-linked. However, after the death, some no longer feel the need to remain silent.

- What has helped you remember realistically?

- Is it unhealthy to create edited versions of relationships with the deceased?

- Are there times when this is necessary? In what circumstances?

Death is a common theme in the Bible. In the Sermon on the Mount, Jesus declared, "Blessed are those who mourn" (Matthew 5:4). This sounds paradoxical. How can anyone in mourning be "blessed"? But Jesus said this to people who were quite acquainted with the raw realities of life and were not into the sophisticated denial of death we practice today.

Jesus added, "for they will be comforted." He promised, not to eliminate death, but to diffuse the power of death. Jesus promised comfort for our darkest moments. Jesus told us that we are going to mourn—no exemptions for his followers—but that when we do, we will be comforted.

- What comes to mind when you hear the word "comforted"?

- In what ways can a griever be comforted?

- Who has been your biggest source of comfort?

- In the margin, list five ways you have been comforted since the death.

It is important for us to review the details of the death. Some of us were on emotional autopilot at the time of the death or funeral; some of us were fatigued because the death came after a long illness. We missed the funeral emotionally and spiritually. We have real difficulty adequately remembering the details. Months or even years after the death we still have large memory gaps. At times we have to request, "Refresh my memory." Sometimes people emphasize certain details to put themselves in a better or softer light, or to exaggerate their importance to the deceased. "You know, I was the last person to see her" or "to speak to him."

- What details of the death are fuzzy to you?

- Why do you think you have difficulty remembering?

- Did you decide to conceal any details of the death or personal life? From whom? Would you make the same decision again?

Task 2: Review the relationship redemptively

"Oh, they were *so* devoted to each other" or "We were the best of friends" are expressions commonly heard at wakes, visitations, funerals, and memorial services. They can be enormously comforting—if they are accurate. But some family members or friends experienced the relationship differently. Such clichés ignite their anger or guilt.

Take a reality check: not everyone had a great marriage. Some, if honest, have to admit that a more accurate adjective might be mediocre, poor, good, average, and so forth. Friendships can atrophy; any relationship can be strained. The healthiest decision is to admit the reality even if that means grieving for what was not.

■ Ask yourself: What am I pretending not to know about *this* relationship?

a. "I have never told anyone this but when I review my relationship with (name), if I am totally honest, I would have to admit_____."

b. "I have often felt _____ about my relationship or a particular aspect of the relationship."

She had been an activist first lady; she had freely challenged the nation's prejudices. Her husband, the president of the United States, died on April 12, 1945. Then Eleanor stumbled onto a bombshell. Her husband had not been alone at the time of his death. Lucy Mercer Rutherford, who had an affair with Franklin Roosevelt, who had worked for them twenty years earlier, had been with him. Eleanor confronted the Secret Service, "Why was I not told?" She stuffed her feelings and carried out her duties as a grieving wife of a great man. "Behind *my* back," she inwardly fumed. Only after her death—two decades later—did the public learn the details of the incident (Paul F. Boller, Jr., *Presidential Wives*, pages 289, 300).

■ Which one of these statements do you agree with?

a. Clearly, Mrs. Roosevelt treated this relationship and death redemptively.

b. Mrs. Roosevelt was not in a position to demand resolution of her "additional" anguish. After all, it was 1945!

Consider this

To act redemptively can be easier said than done. Sometimes it's hard to genuinely grieve for some people: "They got what was coming to them!"

- Whom would you find it difficult to grieve? Why?

- Sometimes death offers an incredible laboratory for forgiveness.

Some grievers are haunted by the internal accusation, "If only I had done more for (name)." Sometimes we need to forgive ourselves. Sometimes in our grief or fatigue we forget how much we actually did for the deceased.

The story of the conflict between King Saul and David illustrates redemptive grieving. Saul had tried to kill David, had given David's wife to another man in marriage, and had forced David into exile. Yet, after Saul's violent death, David genuinely mourned.

"Then David took hold of his clothes and tore them; and all the men who were with him did the same. They mourned and wept, and fasted until evening for Saul and for his son Jonathan and for the army of the LORD and for the house of Israel, because they had fallen by the sword.... David intoned [a] lamentation over Saul and his son Jonathan" (2 Samuel 1:11-12, 17).

David wanted his people to remember their king redemptively. He was kind in spite of Saul's hostile behavior!

- If you had been in David's shoes, how would you have reacted? Could you have written a song of lament?

At first, some of the newly revealed details or circumstances, some of the new realities, may make it difficult for you to grieve redemptively. It may take some time. Still, it is a choice. Yes, you can mentally convene a grand jury and indict the deceased for every offense, for every blemish. However, that will consume a great deal of your energy.

The sooner you act redemptively, the sooner you can get on with your life.

Consider this

Anne Sexton can help us understand redemptive grief with this sentence, "It doesn't matter who my father was; it matters who I remember he was." (See Amy Dean, *Proud to Be*, June 14.) Take a moment and test Sexton's words. Substitute the relationship you are grieving for "father" in her sentence.

- Do you agree or disagree with the rephrased statement?

- How have you acted redemptively toward your dead?

- How have you acted toward those who may be grieving the same death as you, but in a different way?

Sometimes it is after you assume that the death is resolved that details come to light that challenge our ability to continue to act redemptively. Almost as if new evidence has surfaced in a murder case, we want to reopen our grief. For example, our culture looks the other way when widowers start dating or even marry soon after a wife's death. We no longer expect widowers to mourn for a year.

Living realistically and redemptively may be difficult in the area of disputed memories. Not everyone recalls events, details, or circumstances the same because memories are filtered through a grid of individuality.

Ellen's story underscores the differences that can arise over memories. She says that as her husband of forty-eight years was dying, he told each of their grown children, "Take care of your mother." The children, however, insist the phrase was, "*Look after* your mother." Ellen sulks, "Do they 'take care' of me? No! They are 'too busy' for their mother!" Incredible tension has developed in the family because of a disputed memory.

Read and discuss.

Consider this

In some families, the issue is regret-based memories. A woman named Mildred remembers, "I feel so guilty because I was not there when Mom died. It was late at night and I had just stepped down the hall for a soft drink and when I came back she was gone. I would never have left if I had thought she would die. Then my sister—who hardly ever helped with Mom—had the nerve to say, 'Why did you leave her?'!"

■ From your experience, what redemptive advice could you offer Mildred?

Read and discuss as a group.

Herb started dating three months after his wife died of a prolonged bout with cancer. The woman he dated was much younger than his wife; in fact, only four years older than Herb's oldest daughter, Karen. His three adult children have reacted differently to their father's new relationship:

Karen: "Mom has only been dead for three months! He must not have loved her if he can take up with this woman so soon after Mom's death."

Tim: "Dad is an adult and I'm not getting into this!

Meredith: "If it makes Dad happy, great! He and Mom had a good marriage and I can understand how he misses that!"

Try improvising the roles in this family. Find volunteers to take the parts of Karen, Tim, and Meredith. Using the three sentences above as a beginning, improvise a family conference.

After a few minutes, the group can complicate the storyline.

■ Suppose the young woman has three small children?

■ Suppose Herb's elderly mother-in-law lives in his house?

■ How do individual memories get in the way of saying yes to new relationship potentials?

Task 3: Review the relationship responsively

The benefit of faith is that we can bring regrets to God. We can ask for forgiveness for our reality-based regrets, and we can ask God to give us grace to confront our imagined regrets. We can also ask for wisdom to diffuse the negative impact of exaggerated regrets, particularly those being laid on us by others.

▓ Pause for a few moments of silence. Perhaps you can ask God to help you "reframe" certain regrets or memories. This is a healthy first step.

Reframing our regrets may mean that we will need to talk out openly our differences with family, friends, or others directly involved, so that we can get on with the resolution of our grief.

Experience your grief. One reason some do not want to deal with memories is that they are so linked with feelings. When situations appear unresolvable, the tension further contributes to the discomfort, and we shut down. However, by our decision not to confront the painful memories actively, we block other family members or friends from working through their own issues.

"There's nothing I can do about it now!" is often an excuse for not working on unresolved grief issues. But this excuse is not accurate. You always have choices. They can speed or derail the grief process. Coming to this grief group is one positive choice you have made; talking to family or friends about unresolved issues can be another. Some people might choose to work with skilled psychologists or counselors. Such healthy choices are ways of actively grieving rather than passively grieving. While you are not responsible for the death, you are responsible for the choices you make in responding to the loss.

Healthy grief begins with a decision: I can realistically, redemptively, and responsively recollect and reexperience my loss.

"Can a loss be mastered by forgetting the past or by embalming it? No! But by extracting from it the essential elements we can nurture our futures without the one we love(d)."

▓ What in this statement about forgetting or embalming the past prompts you to respond, "Oh, yes!"

▓ What causes you to say, "Oh, no!"?

Wrap-up

Before you go, take time for the following:

- Group ministry task

- Review

- Personal concerns and prayer concerns

- Closing prayers

Daily walk

Bible readings

Day 1
Psalm 34:15-19

Day 2
Psalm 31:7-10

Day 3
1 Thessalonians 4:13-18

Day 4
Genesis 35:16-21

Day 5
Genesis 35:27-29

Day 6
Job 7:6-16

Day 7
2 Corinthians 1:3-7

Thought for the journey

"Blessed are those who grieve realistically, redemptively, and responsively, for they will be comforted." That's one paraphrase of Jesus' words in Matthew 5:4. If you like, take a moment and compose your own paraphrase.

Prayer for the journey

God, give me the courage to recollect and reexperience my loss. Give me strength to be realistic, redemptive, and responsive in this season of grief. Amen.

Verse for the journey

"Blessed are those who mourn, for they will be comforted" (Matthew 5:4).

4 Relinquishing the Old Attachments

The fourth healthy choice is to relinquish old attachments, to the deceased and to the old assumptive world.

Community building

Option

Using construction paper and markers, make two warning or welcoming signs (examples: "I'm Grieving: No Trespassing" or "Please Wait for An Invitation"). The signs can say: 1) what you want to tell others now; and 2) what you hope to tell others when you are more able to reach out to them. Talk together about your signs.

Number off by one and two around the group. Form a line of ones with a line of twos facing them. Let the ones lace their fingers tightly together. Twos will attempt to pull the ones' fingers apart. On the next attempt, the ones can decide if they will resist or cooperate. Finally, the ones and twos switch roles and try again.

This illustrates the issue of strength. Few people can pull the fingers apart unless the partner cooperates. Likewise, with grief, your ties to the deceased can be so strong that no one will ever break them without your cooperation. You can build a new future only by releasing your grasp on the past to reach out to the potential for new relationships.

Opening prayer

Savior, you have promised to be with us even to the end of the world. This death feels like the end of the world to us. Are we safe in assuming that you will be with us even to the end of our grief? Help us to consider the links with the deceased that we need to relinquish. Amen.

We live in a culture that doesn't value the grief process. Who has time to thoroughly grieve? The culture insists, "Get over it! You've got a life to live! Life goes on."

"Ten days after my seventeen-year-old son was murdered, I went back to work. My supervisor walked up and said, 'Glad to see you got this out of your system.' I stood there in shock. How could he say that to me? How can my son's death be summed up in one word: 'this'? At least he could have said, 'I'm sorry.'"

—Bill

People say stupid things to the grieving, but they think—without verbalizing—even stupider things.

- What is the stupidest thing anyone has said to you during your grief? Recall particularly what people have said about the way you are or are not grieving.

- Has anyone suggested that it's time you get over your loss?

- Have you experienced any nonverbal suggestions?

Grief is an individual pattern, yet the Jewish faith has established guidelines for grieving. The seven-day period following a death is called *shiva*. The daily life of a mourner is restricted during this community-recognized period. For thirty days (eleven months for parents) the *kaddish* prayer is recited during prayer services. One year after the death, mourners gather to unveil the grave marker, a gathering which formally concludes the active mourning.

Outside the Jewish community these days, you are pretty much on your own as a griever. Individual family members or other friends may greatly vary on how much time and energy they allocate to active mourning.

However, there comes a time—in order to be spiritually and emotionally healthy—when the griever has to relinquish the loss in order to accept the gift of a future. Remember that early dawn after Jesus' death when the women took the spices to the tomb and found only two men in dazzling clothes? The question the men asked the startled women is a good question for grievers today: "Why do you look for the living among the dead?" (Luke 24:5).

- Do people look for you among the living or among the dead?

Task 1: Inventory your attachments

Explore and relate.

Look around your life, your home, your office, your car, for all that still links you to the deceased. Identify those links under the headings below. Include abstract (non-physical) as well as tangible (physical) links. If you are willing, share part or all of your list with the group.

Tangible items could include such things as a home, lake property, automobiles, furniture, children, stocks, jewelry, art, hobbies, collectibles, or even sexual expression. *Abstract* items could include: faith heritage, memories, reputation in the community, or mourning style.

Tangible	Abstract
_____	_____
_____	_____
_____	_____
_____	_____
_____	_____
_____	_____

Take, for example, an automobile parked in your garage. As the estate is settled, that car will be appraised. It could be a junker, economically of little value, but oh, the emotional attachment. Should you relinquish it? Eventually you will need to replace a car. What kind of car will you, the surviving spouse, buy? Some spouses, even though dead, have been able to dictate selection.

Few items will be as critical as a wedding band. How long do you continue to wear it? After a long marriage, you may feel naked without it. What do you do with it? Bottom drawer? Safe-deposit box?

After the death of a spouse or child, at what point do you put away some or many or all of the pictures? Notice the difference between "put away" and "give away." What about personal objects?

Discovery

Task 2: Honor your ambivalence

Read and discuss as a group.

The only rule in relinquishing is this: relinquish at your own pace. Certainly, the advice-givers will not hesitate to offer suggestions, perhaps with the best of intentions. Listen to them. Consider their suggestions. But make your own decisions.

When reading Scripture, it is often critical to read to the end of the passage, as in John 11, the story of Lazarus's illness and death.

John 11:38-44

[38]Then Jesus, again greatly disturbed, came to the tomb. It was a cave, and a stone was lying against it. [39]Jesus said, "Take away the stone." Martha, the sister of the dead man, said to him, "Lord, already there is a stench because he has been dead four days." [40]Jesus said to her, "Did I not tell you that if you believed, you would see the glory of God?" [41]So they took away the stone. And Jesus looked upward and said, "Father, I thank you for having heard me. [42]I knew that you always hear me, but I have said this for the sake of the crowd standing here, so that they may believe that you sent me." [43]When he had said this, he cried with a loud voice, "Lazarus, come out!" [44]The dead man came out, his hands and feet bound with strips of cloth, and his face wrapped with strips of cloth. Jesus said to them, "Unbind him, and let him go."

- In this passage, what catches your attention?

- What was Martha's possible motive for mentioning the stench?

- What tone of voice (rebuke, chagrin) might Jesus have used to say, "Did I not tell you. . . ."?

- What comes to mind with John's words, "Jesus, again greatly disturbed..."?

- How might Jesus have looked and sounded? Demonstrate how you think Jesus acted and sounded at the time.

After Jesus raised Lazarus from the dead, a crucial detail remained: Lazarus was still bound in grave-clothes. Why did not Jesus himself "unbind him, and let him go"? Because Jesus wanted others to participate in the miracle. That principle is still valid. In a sense, many of us who grieve get tied up as well in the grave clothes.

We too need someone to free us, someone to help us relinquish. In the case of a spouse or child, some want to embalm the relationship or preserve the possessions to nurture a fantasy. Some resist any idea of changing a bedroom and take pride in noting, "Everything is just as she/he left it."

- From your experience with "unbinding grave clothes," how would you counsel someone who wants to embalm possessions?

- What would you say to someone who wants to become a museum operator rather than an active griever?

If the process of relinquishing is disturbing, you may need to question the pace. It may be too much, too soon. Some people do step-by-step relinquishing. For example, they may move personal items out of a bedroom. Yet they are not ready to call the Salvation Army to come and pick up the items. So the items to be relinquished go to a holding area: in boxes in the garage or the basement. These steps are small, but they still lead toward healthy relinquishing.

Jackie Kennedy was a role model of grief for many, although some certainly consider her stoic "whatever you do, don't let them see you cry" approach unhealthy. She gave Pierre Salinger, President Kennedy's longtime press aide, a leather cigar case, which held only two cigars, and the following note of appreciation for his loyalty to her husband: "For dear Pierre. I know you carry more cigars than this, but I thought you might like to have this cigar case that belonged to Jack. It comes with all my love and appreciation for all you did to make his days here so unforgettable." ("Remembering Jackie," *Town and Country*, page 62). Relinquishing became an early priority for her.

As a mother with two small children, however, Jackie Kennedy did not relinquish the stories. Theodore H. White reported that she invited old Kennedy confidantes, such as himself, to dinner to tell stories about their father to Caroline and John. (Editors of *Life*, *Remembering Jackie: A Life in Pictures*.)

Discovery

Task 3: Make relinquishing a priority, not an obsession

Read and discuss.

Ask for assistance. In the case of small children, it could be years before they can appreciate possessions of a parent or grandparent. As an antique buff, I now grieve for items I see in antique stores that remind me of items my grandparents had. However, as a teenager at the time they died, I put no value on their household goods.

Nurture yourself during the relinquishing. It is hard emotional work. Talk to family, friends, or a counselor. Ask for help with the sorting and packing. Write in a journal. Pray as you pack and sort. Remember to save an item for a close friend of the deceased.

Often through prayer and silence, we make good decisions. James 1:5 says, "If any of you is lacking in wisdom, ask God, who gives to all generously and ungrudgingly, and it will be given you."

- Mark any words or phrases in that verse that leap out at you.

- In your grief, what is a particular situation that you could pray for wisdom?

- The phrase or word that speaks to my situation is _____ because_____.

If you open your relinquishing process to God, you will find answers or ideas that would never have occurred to you. The prayer could be: "God, what shall (should, could) I do with (name the object)?"

Be prepared for guidance. Remember that relinquishing the intangible can be as difficult as giving up objects of art or clothes. Jesus experienced relinquishing. Because the Bible does not mention Joseph after the return from Jerusalem, many scholars assume that Joseph had died, and that his death may have been one reason Jesus did not start his ministry until he was thirty. "When Jesus [hanging on the cross] saw his mother and the disciple whom he loved standing by her," he, in essence, relinquished her into John's care. He said, "Woman, here is your son," and to John, "Here is your mother" (John 19:26-27).

You may need to relinquish the endless repetition of the details of the death. You may need to relinquish blaming a doctor for not correctly diagnosing or treating your loved one, or the loved one for not following those orders. You may need to relinquish indicting persons who were not there for you during the early days of your grieving.

If you are male, you may need to relinquish your "I'm doing fine" image. Many males sabotage healing because they insist on modeling the "John Wayne, I am macho, I can take it!" grief style. I remember how strong Richard Nixon was when he resigned the presidency; but I was deeply moved by his honest releasing of his anguish at the burial of Mrs. Nixon. He wept.

You may need to relinquish your endless evaluating of the last days, weeks, or months of the deceased's life, particularly if she or he was in great pain. Some grievers keep placing actions, words, and attitudes under the microscope.

Yes, there may come a time to relinquish the eternal flame of your devotion to the deceased.

- What keeps some of us from relinquishing? Write some answers in the margin.

Read and discuss.

Consider this

What keeps us from relinquishing? "Partly, no doubt, vanity. We want to prove to ourselves, that we are lovers on the grand scale, tragic heroes; not just ordinary privates in the huge army of the bereaved, slogging along and making the best of a bad job."

C.S. Lewis, *A Grief Observed*, page 63.

- What have you tried to prove through your grief?

- To whom have you tried to prove your love?

The apostle Paul recognized that Christians were vulnerable to spiritual attack during the season of grief. There comes a moment, Paul writes in Ephesians, "so that you may be able..., having done everything, to stand firm" (6:13). Indeed, there will come a moment when—just as you have relinquished possessions and art and clothes—you will slowly close the door and relinquish your grief.

No one would suggest that relinquishing your attachments to the deceased will be easy work. However, it is necessary work.

Wrap-up

Before you go, take time for the following:

- Group ministry task

- Review

- Personal concerns and prayer concerns

- Closing prayers

Daily walk

Bible readings

Day 1
Ephesians 6:10-18

Day 2
Ruth 1:3-5; 20-21

Day 3
Deuteronomy 30:15-20

Day 4
2 Thessalonians 2:16-17, 3:1-3

Day 5
Philippians 4:4-8

Day 6
Psalm 139:1-7

Day 7
Psalm 138:6-8

Thought for the journey

Blessed are those who relinquish, who learn to let go. Blessed are those who unwrap the grave clothes so that those who grieve can live.

Prayer for the journey

God, if we let go, aren't we abandoning (name)? Give us the grace to adequately relinquish so that our hearts can be open to a future without this one who so shaped our past and our present. Amen.

Verse for the journey

"The dead man came out, his hands and feet bound with strips of cloth, and his face wrapped in a cloth. Jesus said to them, 'Unbind him, and let him go'" (John 11:44).

5 Readjusting to a New World

The fifth healthy choice toward healing after a significant death is to readjust and to move adaptively to the new world without forgetting the old.

Community building

Option

Go around the group and as the leader says each person's name, mention one word that comes to mind when you think of this person, or one word you would want to give this person to take from the session.

Take a few moments, in silence, to look at the individuals with whom you have shared these sessions. Think about what you've learned about each person's grief, and about what in their experience with grief has touched or affected your own journey.

As the facilitator goes around the group, naming each person, share some of your thoughts with the group. Allow about two minutes for your comments.

Opening prayer

Renewer, although we prefer life the way it was, you do not invite us to the past but do invite us to readjust to a new world without this one whom we have loved. You invite us to a new definition of ourselves. Help us to adapt, confident of your support, grace, and love. Amen.

Read and discuss as a group.

"You should know that your life mattered and that the world around you was changed because you passed this way."

Noela N. Evans, *Meditations for the Passages and Celebrations of Life*, page 10.

Many people are not as afraid of death or of dying as of being forgotten. It is one thing to know or to be told, "Your life mattered and the world was changed by your birth." However, it is equally important to know that the world was changed by one's passing as well. When I die, I want people at the grave crying, "How are we going to live without Harold?" not back at McDonald's drinking coffee and eating a Danish!

The little phrase "to move adaptively into the new world" reminds us that grief recovery is a choice. It is not so much what happens to us but how we choose to respond. The choices one makes in a grief journey ultimately determine the duration and impact of grief.

■ In the margin, list five positive choices you have made as a result of this significant death.

What choices have you come to regret? My laptop computer has a wonderful option, "undo." When I have slapped my forehead and screamed, "Oh no!" it is so comforting to jump to the edit menu and undo what I have just deleted. Too bad life isn't like that. Or is it? Redeeming earlier choices becomes possible when we revise our old world and its assumptions, develop a new relationship with the deceased, and form a new identity.

■ Have you ever experienced an opportunity to redeem an earlier choice?

Task 1: Revise the old world and its assumptions

Read and discuss.

The movie *Schindler's List* tells about one man's attempt to save Jewish lives during World War II. In one disturbing but typical scene, the commandant of the camp fired indiscriminately at the inmates, killing them as they walked to their jobs.

Two elderly women were killed on a Sunday night two blocks from my front door. They had walked out of a Bible study and were accosted by two men who robbed them and killed them. In *my* neighborhood! Coming out of a Bible study! At the time this happened, I had just pulled into my driveway and was unloading my car after returning home from a speaking engagement. It could have been me!

We all live with assumptions about the way things are supposed to be. That's a great word: *supposed.*

"I always thought that I would die first. She was not supposed to go first. How can I live without her?"

> —John, sixty-seven, after the sudden death of his wife.

"Children are supposed to bury their parents—not the other way around."

> —Karen, after death of 17-year-old daughter.

"He had the best medical attention in the world. It was supposed to be routine. 'Not to worry' the doctor had told us."

> —Beth, on her husband's death at age 29.

■ Can anyone in the group share a story with a "supposed to" element?

Every "supposed to" is based on an assumption which often includes a lot of feelings about God. Some of God's field reps only complicate grief with such statements as, "It (the death) was God's will" or God "allowed" the death. The speakers hope to soften our frustrations about God but don't answer our real questions, according to Daniel J. Simundson (*Where Is God In My Suffering?*, page 53).

Some people don't mince words in offering a different answer: "That is evident! You didn't have enough faith!" Or "God took your son to test your faith."

"I sat there, two months after my daughter died, listening to this person give a testimony about how she had prayed and God had spared her son's life. I wanted to cuss. 'Just trust God,' she said. So how come God didn't answer my prayers?"

> —George

■ How would you have responded to such a statement early in your bereavement?

■ How would you respond now?

■ What other "God talk" answers have you been offered?

I was rocked to the core by the death of my 18-year-old friend Denny, college freshman, solid, handsome, bright, the oldest son of one of my best friends. Denny died by the fireplace in the family room one morning—of mononucleosis. Mono is not supposed to kill college students. Mono killed Denny. Late one night, after spending the day trying to console my grief-stricken friends, I dared voice, "God, you have some explaining to do on this one!" To this day, I still feel a Denny-shaped hole in my heart. If there was a quota on teenage males that day, why not some drug dealer? Why an all-American kid with his whole life ahead of him? Can anybody understand?

There are mounds of unprocessed God-anger in the grief landscapes of many of us. Many of us don't dare verbalize our pain, our disappointment, fearing the other shoe will drop. Often in a landscape called grief we must come to terms with our inadequate understandings of God. God is not the big C.E.O. in the sky controlling everything and everybody. Our anger does not intimidate God. Our minds are too small to understand all that we have questions about. But we know we live in a broken world, and much that happens is not God's will. Some mysteries will not be explained during our time on earth, but we do know that the ultimate victory over death has already been accomplished. God can handle our anger. As my friend Reg Johnson says, "God never chides his children for being children."

- Have you ever dared to verbalize your God-anger?

- By doing so, did you make anyone uncomfortable?

Consider this

Some questions only get silence. Keep asking! Let the questions live!

The question "How could a good God let this happen?" is huge. Some of you might be interested in reading more. Among the many helpful books on the subject are *Where Is God in My Suffering?* by Daniel Simundson, mentioned earlier, and Douglas John Hall, *God and Human Suffering.* Turn to the "Resources" list on page 78 for more information on these titles.

A further look

"My God, my God, why have you forsaken me? Why are you so far from helping me, from the words of my groaning? O my God, I cry by day, but you do not answer; and by night, but find no rest" (Psalm 22:1-2).

Psalmists were not shy with their questions. Reread this passage carefully.

- What words leave the impression that the psalmist is acquainted with grief?

- Take one of the psalmist's questions and rephrase it in your own words.

Discovery

Task 2: Develop a new relationship with the deceased

Explore and relate.

It happens, often among long-married couples. One dies and within weeks, months at most, the other dies. Sometimes, particularly among the childless elderly, the death of one totally eliminates the social support system of the other.

As a funeral director, I had a client who wanted to have a fresh, long-stemmed rose placed on his wife's grave every day—as a testimony to his love. He had the money, and a florist was willing, but I had to wonder about the motivation. Who was getting something out of this, other than the florist? Was the husband making his love into a legend? Was he atoning for what he had not given her during her lifetime?

- Some of us do want to get our niche in the Grievers' Hall of Fame. What would it take for you to be inducted?

A person enters a second arena of pain when he or she remarries prematurely without having done adequate grief work.

Many second spouses have explained, "It's hard to compete with a ghost." Indeed, some people will go to elaborate lengths to preserve their protected image of a deceased spouse.

- What are some of the obstacles to a new relationship?

In some cases uncovering "secrets" (sexual orientation, alcoholism, child abuse, an affair, or a gambling addiction), particularly when a reality shatters a well-polished public identity, complicates the grieving process. One feminist struggled with her post-funeral shock at discovering that her father's business printed pornography. Some have been shocked to learn of another romantic relationship, or even children by other relationships.

Susan's husband, a respected church leader, died HIV-positive. The AIDS virus had been transmitted sexually in a relationship with someone else. The undisclosed part of her grief ties her to a false relationship with the deceased; they had only an appearance of a marriage.

In the Jewish faith, the eulogy is balanced with what is called *hesped*, the expectation "to tell the truth about the person who has died and about the loss and its emotional consequences" (Anne Brener, *Mourning & Mitzvah*, page 25). Indeed, Jewish people believe that those who bear false witness at a funeral— and those who knowingly say amen to the false witness—will be called to give account for their falsehood. The attempt to eulogize the dead—and overlook big chunks of reality—makes healing difficult if not impossible.

Not everyone will choose to disclose the full extent of their wound to family or friends; some will find the path to healing though work with a skilled counselor or psychologist with whom raw grief feelings can be processed or refined.

Sometimes we must declare our grief in the same way as the ancient mourner, Job: "I will not restrain my mouth; I will speak in the anguish of my spirit; I will complain in the bitterness of my soul" (Job 7:11).

That last sentence could be translated, "I will give voice to my grief." But honesty will not make everyone happy; some are content to work overtime to keep up illusions of the deceased. Bildad the Shuhite, supposedly Job's friend, challenged him, "How long will you say these things, and the words of your mouth be a great wind?" (8:2). Sometimes grief, as Frank Sinatra used to sing, has to be done "my way."

- ▓ What questions did you avoid asking the deceased or asking about the deceased among family or friends?

- ▓ What are you pretending not to know about your relationship with the deceased?

Sometimes, one has to let go of the old reality in order to embrace the healthy new reality. Your loved one is dead!

Task 3: Adopt new ways of being in the world

Read aloud.

Instead of saying "new ways of being in the world," perhaps we should say "new ways of being fully present in the world." Some people experience a longer gap between death and burial than two or three days; some experience a gap of years.

As a child, I was somewhat horrified by pictures from foreign countries of wives being burned on funeral pyres with the bodies of their deceased husbands. Although we do not have physical pyres in this culture, we do have emotional ones. It takes work to move away from being consumed by the past and toward creating a new future.

After Stella's husband died, she did the mourning thing, then she set to work establishing a new reality. Her first decision was to have lots of light, lots of color, lots of music, and lots of good smells in her home. Because of her husband's alcoholism and violent temper, years had passed since guests had been in her home. Immediately, she began inviting people for desserts and eventually for meals. She told her pastor, "You pick out five newcomers to our church and come with them. I will fix Sunday brunch." Stella spent late Sunday afternoons visiting patients in area hospitals who had few visitors. "I am sorry he died," she admitted. "I am sorry we lost the good years of his life. I am not sure how many years I have left, but I can guarantee you this: I will know zest." Hundreds of widows and widowers in her town have received a phone call or visit from Stella with her enthusiastic message of "Live!"

Read and discuss.

Consider this

If you spend your life mourning what could have been, you will waste what could be!

Certainly, you open yourself to criticism with your healthy choices to live with zest. One woman bought a sporty convertible soon after her husband's death. "Would Earl (her late husband) approve?" a neighbor challenged her. "Probably not, but then he's not here and I am."

Read aloud and discuss.

Some people, ironically, have come to life only after a spouse's death. Healthy people realize the incredible effect—positive and negative—that the deceased had. One woman addressed these words to her deceased friend, "I think of things I learned from you and hope you know what value they bring to me" (Noela N. Evans, *Meditations*, page 12).

C. Everett Koop, formerly Surgeon General, has expressed great concern for the deaths from AIDS of a generation of young men. Koop's son, David, a junior at Dartmouth, died in a rock climbing accident. Koop knew firsthand a parent's grief when he wrote the following:

"Words are inadequate to describe the depth of our shock, hurt and loss. Losing a child brings a poignant and tender grief unlike any other.... Nothing changed our lives—and the lives of our surviving children—like the death of our son David.... I thought that now I might be better able to help parents of dying children, but for quite a while I felt less able, too emotionally involved" (C. Everett Koop, *Koop: The Memoirs of America's Family Doctor*, page 95-96).

Koop had been taught in his medical training that a physician should never cry with parents of his pediatric patients because parents might see the emotion as a sign of weakness. However, after Koop experienced the death of his child, he lamented, "I could rarely discuss the death of a child without tears welling up into my eyes" (page 96). Koop learned that parents found his tears a strength.

The apostle Paul wrote, "Blessed be the God and Father of our Lord Jesus Christ, the Father of mercies and the God of all consolation, who consoles us in all our affliction" (2 Corinthians 1:3-4a). This is a wonderful promise to those who know grief firsthand. Yet, Paul did not stop with those words but continued, "so that." So that what? "...so that we can may be able to console those who are in any affliction with the consolations with which we ourselves are consoled by God" (1:4b). We assume that we should be self-sufficient in ourselves. God comforts us so that we live a new identity in the world: as fellow grievers. Blessed are those who move adaptively into the new world!

Wrap-up

Before you go, take time for the following:

- Group ministry task

- Review

- Personal concerns and prayer concerns

- Closing prayers

Daily walk

Bible readings

Day 1
Deuteronomy 31:1-8

Day 2
2 Corinthians 12:6-10

Day 3
Job 2:7-13

Day 4
Ephesians 3:14-21

Day 5
Psalm 103:13-18

Day 6
Job 42:10-17

Day 7
Acts 20:32-38; 21:1

Thought for the journey

Blessed are those who readjust to move adaptively into the new world. Blessed are those who respond creatively, redemptively, and resourcefully to the deaths in their lives.

Prayer for the journey

God, you are a companion to us in our grief, give us the courage and strength to move adaptively into our new worlds and new realities, knowing that you will accompany us all the way. Amen.

Verse for the journey

"And the peace of God, which surpasses all understanding, will guard your hearts and your minds in Christ Jesus" (Philippians 4:7).

6 Reaching Out to a New Future

Focus

The sixth healthy choice is to reach out to a new future, not by totally forgetting the past relationship but by remembering the best of the relationship in order to nurture the future.

Community building

Option

Pass an index card around the group. Notice that *PAST TENSE* is printed on one side and *FUTURE TENSE* on the other. Hold up the side that best currently describes you and tell the group why you chose that side. What would it take to get you to future tense?

Scan the list below. Select one item and tell how the death has changed your thinking, choices, and attitude toward the item. If the group is small, each person can select a category and ask everyone to contribute to the discussion on that choice.

a. Eating alone
b. Eating alone in public
c. Faith
d. Going to church alone
e. Spending money
f. Clothes
g. Vacations
h. Holidays

i. Old friends
j. Pets
k. Hobbies
l. Household chores
m. A new relationship
n. Going to events at night
o. My job

Opening prayer

Creator, you invite us to the future where you wait for us. We cannot live creatively in the past but only in the present and in the future. Nudge us, this day, toward our future. Amen.

Choose your future

Read and discuss as a group.

We can expect resistance, perhaps from some who claim to love us most, as we attempt "to transform our relationship with someone who has died from a wound to a blessing" (Anne Brener, *Mourning and Mitzvah*, Woodstock, Vermont: Jewish Lights, 1993, page 135).

While we may not be able to change our realities, we can change the way we remember and interpret our realities, our histories, and our losses. It all comes down to a choice: my choice. You may recall the old saying, "It is not so much what happens to me, but how I choose to respond." How do you—as one who has experienced a significant death and loss—reach out to the future? By forming a new identity, by reinvesting yourself, and by reconciling yourself to the death.

Suppose I were to offer you five hundred dollars to drive me to a speaking assignment. No problem! You would volunteer. What if I added one provision: you would have to cover the windshield and could only use the rearview mirror. Would we go even a block before a crash? Yet many grievers have done just that. They have windshields the size of the rearview mirrors, and memory rearview mirrors the size of windshields. Some are trying to see the future through the tiniest portal.

- Which is larger: your memory rearview mirror or your windshield?

Task 1: Form a new identity

Read and discuss.

Have you ever watched sidewalks being poured? Someone doesn't just start pouring concrete. First, steel or wood forms are laid to frame the design of the sidewalk. The forms become the boundaries for the concrete. Our relationships form the framework for much of our emotional stability. You will continuously have to grapple with the questions, "Who am I without this significant person in my life?" and "What did I do today to build new frames, new boundaries?"

Another part of forming a new identity is to deal with first-person-singular language.

- Has anyone who has lost a spouse had difficulty switching from *we* language to *I* language?

- How have you been verbally reminded of your new status?

- Has anyone who has lost a child struggled when someone asked, "How many children do you have?"

Rabbi Josef Ekstein formed a new identity after the death of his fourth child from Tay-Sachs disease, a genetic disorder from which his first three children had also died. Four deaths! The rabbi could have been bitter; rather he and his wife chose to accept their fate. But they decided to believe that God had given them four children with Tay-Sachs so that they could help other families with children with this genetically-transmitted disease. (Turn back to page 54 and reread 2 Corinthians 1:3-4.)

The Eksteins formed an identity around being helpers rather than grievers. They formed an organization, Dor Yeshorim, to screen young members of their religious community for the gene and to encourage carriers not to pass the gene on to the next generation (Shannon Brownlee, "The Narrowing of Normality," *U.S. News & World Report*, page 67).

Discovery

Task 2: Reach out to other grievers

Read aloud and discuss.

You may not wish to found an organization to reach out. You may decide, as did Beverly Barbo, to speak out and eventually to write about the significant death in her life, her son Tim, from AIDS. Although many choose to shroud a family member's death from the highly-stigmatized illness, Beverly chose to speak out and to reach out so that other parents would not feel as alone and as isolated as she and her husband had felt. Her book, *The Walking Wounded* has touched many lives. Through her appearances, her book, and more importantly her willingness to talk about AIDS issues, her tragedy has made a big difference to many.

Perhaps fifteen hundred miles away from Beverly Barbo's home, the sister of a man who had died of AIDS, having witnessed both bigotry and hysteria throughout her brother's illness, said, "I've got to do something." After reading a newspaper clipping about Beverly, she telephoned her. Beverly encouraged this new griever to get involved. Within months, she was actively involved in a local AIDS support network. Others have found help through organizations like M.A.D.D. and The Compassionate Friends.

> ◼ If you have found help through such an organization, share your experience with the group.

You can also reach out through presence. I saw the AIDS Names Quilt displayed in Sacramento—a sobering experience. I noticed a distraught older woman, seemingly confused, walking slowly along the rows. Before I could offer to assist her, a woman slipped up beside her and asked if she could help.

"I can't find him," the first woman sobbed. "Him" was her thirty-nine-year-old son who had died and had been honored with a panel in the quilt. Rarely have I witnessed such compassion.

"I remember how hard it was when my son died," the second woman said softly. Reaching out her arm to wrap around her new friend, she said, "You're going to make it. I'll help you find your son's panel." When I left the display two hours later the two women, deep in conversation, had barely moved. A mother, well acquainted with grief, gave another grieving mother the gift of "I have been there"—experienced presence.

Explore and relate.

> ◼ Who has offered you experienced presence?

> ◼ To whom have you offered experienced presence?

My friends, Dennis and Buelah, after their son's death, have given chunks of presence to other grieving parents. In one instance, when another young boy was killed in their community, many people went immediately to the residence to express their condolences. As Dennis and Buelah approached the family, the father said, "Now here are some people who understand." Their two sons, although their deaths were two years apart, lie side-by-side in a small Kansas cemetery.

Explore and relate.

> ◼ Who has reached out to you?

> ◼ What was the most effective element in their gifts of compassion in reaching out to you?

> ◼ What gift, if offered at the time of your loss, could have made a difference?

> ◼ Who failed to reach out to you?

> ◼ Have you ever let them know how their failure affected you?

Read and discuss as a
group.

About 4,000 years ago a man named Job—described as
"blameless and upright, one who feared God and turned away
from evil" (Job 1:1)—learned about the role of presence (both
positive and negative) through three self-appointed "com-
forters" who came calling on him.

One calamity after another had hit Job. His oxen and donkeys
were stolen, fire burned his sheep, a group of raiders took his
camels, and virtually all of his servants were killed. Finally, he
received the message that his sons and daughters had sud-
denly been killed. His friends arrived to console him, but
"when they saw him from a distance, they did not recognize
him, and they raised their voices and wept aloud; they tore
their robes and threw dust in the air upon their heads. They
sat with him on the ground seven days and seven nights, and
no one spoke a word to him, for they saw that his suffering
was very great" (Job 2:12-13).

- Have you ever felt such a loss of words? You knew you
  should say something but could not find the words?

- Have you ever spoken, then regretted the words as soon
  as they were spoken?

- What do you think motivates us to "say something"
  when we think we should improve on the gift of silence?

In Jewish condolence customs, visitors are not expected to say
anything—just be there. Sometimes presence can be annoying;
especially if guests start pontificating as did Job's trio.

- Have any of you experienced an unusual or daring, but
  still comforting, gift of presence? Share it with the group.

- Have you ever initiated the gift of presence in this manner? Tell the group.

Discovery

Task 3: To reconcile the loss

Read and discuss.

One vulgar expression is common after a death. Four simple
words (often punctuated with an exclamation mark) have an
almost infinite capacity to further wound and to inhibit or
hamstring the grief process: "You'll get over it!"

One woman told me that those were the first words "of comfort" a hospital chaplain offered her after her husband was
pronounced dead. Some comfort! Perhaps you have even
heard the phrase turned into an order, "Get over it!"

Do a reality check: No, you won't get over it. Ever. The wounded don't get over a loss. Sadly, in our culture thousands of people have spent a lifetime trying to get over a death or to get on with life. Some have layers of deaths, each fresh death knocking off the scabs from the previous unhealed ones.

You won't get over it, but if you choose—four more key words—you can become reconciled to the loss.

A young Army couple stationed in Maryland lost their first-born son, three-year-old David, to scarlet fever in 1920. The father was not allowed in his son's bedroom because of the quarantine. He would go to the screen window of the boy's bedroom and push his face into that screen and talk to his son. Fighting for emotional control, he broken-heartedly watched his son sink into a coma and finally die the day after Christmas. The young couple was told: "You'll get over it"—four words offered to many couples—and "You'll have another child" (Stephen A. Ambrose, *Eisenhower: Soldier and President*, page 38).

Years went by. In the desert of North Africa, when notified of his father's death back in Kansas, he chose not to request leave. The enlisted men couldn't go home for funerals, so why should he? He finally pulled down his tent flap and asked to be left alone for a while with his loss.

Dwight David Eisenhower never "got over it" and neither will you. He did reconcile himself to his loss. Will you? Or will you be too busy as director of the museum of the deceased?

First do this individually, then talk together.

Consider this

"One never loses memories of a significant relationship." The task is to find "an appropriate place for the dead in [our] emotional lives—a place that will enable [us] to go on living effectively in the world."

J. William Worden, *Grief Counseling & Grief Therapy*, pages 16-17.

■ What is the key word for you in Worden's observation?

Discuss as a group.

Earlier we read about Job's losses, and his friends' misguided attempts to comfort him. We learn that, "In all this (and Job had more than his fair share of *this*), Job did not sin by charging God with wrong-doing" (1:22). Amazing! Most of us could not have suffered such losses and followed Job's script! Nor would some of the psalmists.

It is not a sin to yell at God or to refuse to acknowledge God or to blame God. Perhaps you still feel guilty and think you have sinned for some of your thoughts and words during your loss. Perhaps you feel guilty because you have not grieved like a spouse or other family members. Mrs. Job, for example, did not grieve in sync with her husband. In fact, she snarled, "Curse God and die" (2:9), a suggestion Job dismissed as "foolish" although death would have released them from their pain. Yet she did not bottle up her grief.

What can you make of Job 42:12, "The Lord blessed the latter days of Job's life more than his beginning"? After ten deaths, Job was blessed beyond his ability to comprehend. Seven sons and three "beautiful" daughters were icing on the cake but even on good days he must have missed those first children.

Maybe this altered paraphrase of Job 1:21 is more on the mark: "The Lord has taken away, the Lord gives. Blessed be the name of the Lord."

William V. Pietsch said it well. "God is going to be continually working to bring about what is best for us as individuals in a complicated world. I can trust a God who is moving me toward a healing" (William V. Pietsch, *The Serenity Prayer Book*, page 66).

Explore and relate. Discuss what God is up to in your life.

To the last sentence, I would add "...and toward reconciliation with the loss." God requires our cooperation. Reading Job 2, we could never imagine Job 42. In hearing your story can we imagine that good will come, in time, after your loss? God is up to something good in your life.

Read and discuss.

Consider this

"One benchmark of a completed grief reaction is when the person is able to think of the [deceased] person without pain. Mourning is finished when a person can reinvest his or her emotions back into life and in the living."

J. William Worden, *Grief Counseling & Grief Therapy*, page 18.

Read aloud and discuss.

So, we have come to the end of our time together of considering six choices—choices that every griever in this group must confront. Take a moment to review the list, then circle the appropriate answer in the left column. Remember this: it is OK to be in "no" or "unsure" categories. Wherever we are is OK.

- Have I recognized my losses?

    Yes   No   Unsure

- Have I reacted authentically, accurately, and adequately to my losses?

    Yes   No   Unsure

- Have I recollected and reexperienced my losses?

    Yes   No   Unsure

- Have I relinquished the old attachments?

    Yes   No   Unsure

- Have I readjusted adaptively to my new world?

    Yes   No   Unsure

- Have I reached out to a new future?

    Yes   No   Unsure

The "Naming of Names" service (pages 73-74) can be done in your last session or at another designated time.

The difference between what I am and what I become is what I choose!

- Are there choices you need to make?

- Share them with the group, if you are willing.

- What would you need for a "let go moment"—a time when you ask God to give you grace to let go of the past in order to embrace the future?

Wrap-up

Before you go, take time for the following:

- Group ministry task

- Review

- Personal concerns and prayer concerns

- Closing prayers

Daily walk

Bible readings

Day 1
Psalm 109:22-27

Day 2
Genesis 37:23-35

Day 3
Philippians 4:6-9

Day 4
Genesis 28:10-17

Day 5
Philippians 3:8-14

Day 6
Revelation 21:1-4

Day 7
John 11:17-26

Thought for the journey

Blessed are those who reach out to a new future. Blessed are those who live creatively in the present. Blessed are those who have learned to live without answers to their questions.

Prayer for the journey

God, lead me to a "let go" moment. Help me recognize the ways you are leading me toward healing and toward reconciliation with my loss. Thank you for a wonderful gift called healthy grieving. Amen.

Verse for the journey

"For surely I know the plans I have for you, says the LORD, plans for your welfare and not for harm, to give you a future with hope" (Jeremiah 29:11).

Facilitator helps

"Deposits of unfinished grief reside in more American hearts than I ever imagined. Until these pockets are opened and their contents aired openly they block unimagined amounts of human growth and potential. They can give rise to bizarre and unexplainable behavior while causing untold internal stress."

Robert Kavanaugh, *Facing Death*, page 82.

As you act as the facilitator for a small group on grief, you will be helping the grieving members unblock their growth and release some of their potential. Given our death-denying culture, you and the group are taking a courageous step as you look realistically at grief and deal with it.

Susanne St. Yves observed: "Society is not comfortable with death. Grieving people find this out quickly. Our whole world plunges into darkness and few people come searching for us with flashlights" ("Lights in the Darkness," page 44).

In essence, you and your group become emotional flashlights to offer support to grieving individuals. What are the assumptions in offering a small group on grief?

- That grief and loss are a vital part of life.

- That listening leads to healing.

- That each griever needs a *mehom hanekhma*, a place of comfort.

- That each griever has a story that needs to be told and heard.

- That answers and explanations are rare.

Is this small group a therapy group?

This grief small group is *not* a therapy group; it does not allow members to pop-psychologize other participants; and it will not meet for an infinite time.

Why is this not an ongoing group?

This group has a starting point and an ending point. You may wish to extend it beyond six sessions, but that would need to be planned ahead of time (see page 72 below).

It is essential that you as the facilitator understand that some may come with their own or a hidden agenda. You must be vigilant in protecting the group. Some people unfortunately do not want to reconcile with their grief but wish to stay tied to what was rather than face the adventure of what could be.

What is "normal" in grief and mourning?

We should begin by noting what Erich Lindemann has identified as five characteristics of normal grief reaction. (See "Symptomatology and Management of Acute Grief," pages 141-148.)

1. Sensations of somatic distress which can be triggered by thinking about or hearing the name of the deceased. These include choking, tightness in the throat, a need to sigh, or what Lindemann calls "intense subjective distress."

2. An intense preoccupation with the image of the deceased, often accompanied by a slight sense of unreality. Grievers may say, "I can't stop thinking about Joan."

3. A feeling of guilt with exaggerated memories of evidence of failure to have done right by the deceased.

4. Hostility, irritability, anger, or annoyance especially with people who intrude and disrupt their grief.

5. A loss of usual patterns of conduct and daily life, such as sleep patterns and eating, or inability to sit still or concentrate.

One benefit of the small group for many will be the discovery that these realities are common among grievers. A "You, too?" feeling will create some relief for many. Indeed, many will preface comments with, "This may sound weird..." or "I think I am going crazy because...." You need to immediately acknowledge the vulnerability of the individual for disclosing: "Thank you for sharing that with us." Remember that "normal" covers a lot of territory.

What if someone in the group needs psychological help?

That would be good. Participating in this small group may be one leg of a journey to healing. This group may help a participant find the courage to seek counseling.

However, as a facilitator you need to be aware of abnormal bereavement reactions which should not be ignored. Bereavement, like any emotion, can be knowingly or unknowingly distorted, sometimes with devastating consequences. The lists below may be helpful.

Bereavement Reactions

Normal Adaptive

1. Somatic distress
2. Preoccupation with image of the deceased
3. Guilt
4. Hostile reactions
5. Temporary loss of patterns of conduct
6. Temporary appearance of traits of deceased in bereavement.

Abnormal/Maladaptive

1. Psychosomatic reactions: colitis, asthma, rheumatoid arthritis
2. Alteration in relations to family and friends or neighbors
3. Prolonged or unreasonable guilt leading to activities detrimental to one's own social and economic existence
4. Furious hostility against a specific person (a doctor or hospital); repression of hostility leading to a wooden and formal manner resembling schizophrenia
5. Lasting loss of patterns of social interactions; overreaction without a sense of loss
6. Permanent acquisition of symptoms of deceased's last illness

Fawzy I. Fawzy, Nancy W. Fawzy, and Robert O. Pasnau, "Bereavement in AIDS," page 473.

What about the Kübler-Ross death-and-dying grief model?

Elisabeth Kübler-Ross never intended that the stage theory developed in her 1969 book, *On Death and Dying*, be carved into granite. However, many people have suggested that her five stage theory be applied to any and all grief (experienced by people who are dying or grieving) and that they need to be experienced in the order presented. To review, her stages are denial, anger, bargaining, depression, and acceptance, although there are many adaptations and modifications of them.

Research literature does not provide solid support for the stage-based model of grief. Charles A. Corr reported that "more than twenty years [after the theory's initial publication] there still is no confirmation of its validity or reliability." There is no solid evidence that dying or grieving "people actually do move from stage one through stage five" (Charles A. Corr, "Coping with Dying," page 70).

What is the theoretical or philosophical approach in this resource?

The approach in this resource is based on the work of Therese A. Rando ("The Increasing Prevalence of Complicated Mourning," *Omega* 26:1) on the increasing prevalence of "complicated" mourning and on the author's experience as a griever and as a grief group facilitator. Healing is facilitated by three factors: 1) choices, particularly to be an active, rather than passive, griever; 2) the support of others; and 3) one's personal choice to reconcile with the death. Simply, there must come a moment when each griever must decide either to rise up and continue with life or to join the living dead.

This grief group is designed to help the participants see the menu of important grieving decisions (especially "Am I going to actively or passively grieve?"), and to "cheerlead" the participant's healthy decision to reconcile with rather than get over the loss.

At times, you will—in the course of listening to a participant—need to remind the group that grief is very individualistic. "Human grief can be vast and distinctive as the relationship that is severed," (Kavanaugh, *Facing Death*, page 83). The purpose of this group is to help grievers find their appropriate grief path.

In summary, this group can:

- Help grieving people discover that they are not alone

- Teach grieving people that some people can be trusted with the "black-and-blue" details of the loss that others do not want or no longer wish to hear

- Encourage grieving people to honestly express their feelings such as anger, rage, denial, or confusion

- Help people healthily release emotions that have been repressed or shamed

- Offer opportunities to actively grieve

- Help grieving people recognize and process their anger toward God, doctors, and even the deceased

- Help grieving people find companions for the grief path

- Offer grieving people *mekom hanekhma*, a place of comfort and a safe place to actively grieve

What if someone starts crying or breaks down? Good. Tears are, contrary to the culture's notions, healthy. This may be one of the few places a grieving person can or will be encouraged to cry. You will want to say, especially at the first session and maybe at subsequent sessions, that

- this group gives you permission to be yourself;

- this group gives you permission to grieve healthily;

- this group gives you permission to cry, tear up, get emotional;

- this group believes that grief stories are often punctuated by tears.

You may print this list on a handout sheet or ask participants to turn to this page and have the group read it at the beginning of each session.

Having said that, watch that box of tissues! Have tissues available, but let the crying person reach for them. You or others should not hand them out. Dr. Alan Wolfelt reports that 80 percent of people, on being handed a tissue, stop crying ("Understanding Grief").

As a facilitator, give verbal permission to males to cry or break down. One unfortunate consequence of gender rigidity in our culture is that many males are emotionally constipated. If so many significant males in Scripture are reported to have cried (Abraham, Isaac, Jacob, Esau, Jeremiah, David, Ezekiel, Jesus, Paul), it is certainly permissible for males in your group to cry.

What about prayer?

"You'll be in my prayers" comes off to many grievers as just another well-meaning cliché. But if you stop to think about those words, they can be impressive and convey real caring.

You and members of the grief group may sometimes be at a loss to know how to pray. You could pray, "(Name) needs help. Help (name) to know how much you love her/him," or "Help (name) grieve." You might want to try roll call prayers. As facilitator, pray aloud for each participant by name, going down the roster of participants. The roll call can also be done by your group, having them turn to page 75 in this book where your names are written. They can simply pray for each, "Lord, help (name) today/tonight/this week."

Should you contact members during the week?

A brief phone call will often be appreciated as a way of checking their reactions to the first meeting and saying that you hope they are having a better week. If someone shares something that moved them deeply in a session, a brief note from you honoring that sharing would no doubt be appreciated.

Session helps

1 Recognizing Your Loss

Because this is the first meeting of the group, you can expect participants to be anxious. Hey, who wants to volunteer to be a griever? "What are you doing tonight?" "Going to a grief group." "Oh, sounds like fun...." Participants are only here because they have had fresh experiences in the valley of the shadow of death.

"Community Building"

In the "Community Building" exercise, some may balk or be hesitant to fully complete the statement about how the person died, particularly if the cause of death has a social stigma attached to it: AIDS, SIDS, suicide, alcohol-related disease or accident, or drug overdose. Some will wait a session or two (or more) before deciding the group can be trusted with more disclosure. It may be that these suffer more from grief than others because their grief cannot be fully admitted or recognized and therefore cannot be fully mourned.

"Discovery" sections

The overall goal of the session is to persuade participants that they have come to a safe place to grieve. Go through the session, reading and discussing the three "Tasks." Keep the session moving; some "Tasks" will evoke more response or reflection than others.

In Task 3, you can expect some participants to be uncomfortable discussing God. One participant may be angry and say so; a tirade may occur. Don't race in—or allow another participant to race in—to rescue God's reputation. God's role in our suffering will be addressed in Session 5.

Healthy bereavement begins with a full airing of one's feelings, and others may become uncomfortable. Remind the group that the Bible has many examples of people angry with God. You might want to refer to some psalms of lament such as Psalms 22 or 102.

"Wrap-up"

Death and Grief is based on the belief that God comforts us so that we can share the comfort we have received with others. This group can gain much by reaching out beyond its boundaries to individuals or organizations who need assistance.

If your small group is sponsored by a church, consider church tasks for which volunteers are always needed. Ask the group to pick a Sunday (after checking with the church secretary) and serve coffee during the fellowship between or after services. This is a chance to serve the church, as well as by its presence to notify the church of the existence of a small group on grief. Serving coffee offers an opportunity to recruit participants for the next small group on grief.

There is also the option of holding a "Naming of Names" service (see page 73) and opening it up to participation by other members of the church. Anyone who experienced a death could be involved. This grief group would sponsor the event, taking time to talk together about what would be needed to get church response, such as a bulletin insert, poster, or oral announcements. Or the group might want to do the service as part of the last session but also schedule a churchwide service of "Naming the Names" later.

You could close this session by asking the group to stand, join hands, and pray the Lord's Prayer.

2 Reacting to Your Loss

"Community Building"

The "Community Building" exercises are good ways for the group to start to get a handle on loss, and to recall some of the issues they will deal with in this session.

"Discovery" sections

This session focuses on three As: authentic, accurate, and adequate reaction(s) to loss. "Grief style" involves both grieving (internal work) and mourning (external work). Be prepared to spend some time understanding the differences because many of the group, especially younger members, will merely consider the words synonymous. You could use a flip chart or overhead. Write *grief* and let participants offer

definitions; then write *mourn*, again hearing definitions. It is helpful to see the group's definitions side by side for immediate comparison.

Your group may find discussing the differences between male and female grief patterns—particularly as blocks to authentic grieving—lively.

This session will be a great time to discuss "stages." Some participants might be surprised that the Kübler-Ross stages are not a primary focus of the study; refer them to pages 66.

"Wrap-up"

What books on grief have been helpful to group members? Those same books would, no doubt, be helpful to others if available in the church library. Check out the selection of books on grieving in your church library. Then see if members of the group have books they would want to donate, used or new. You can also ask members for recommendations of books and see if there is money in the church library funds for purchasing these resources. Moreover, in this day of video, perhaps videos would be more likely to be used. The group could also ask for members of the church who would like to memorialize a friend or family member through this means. Finally, on a chosen Sunday, members of the small group could do a display of books on grief and be prepared to do mini-recommendations for future reading. This is a little "seed" planted in the minds of the church's members for future reference.

Encourage group members to add sentence prayers to the closing prayer. For example, you could say, "God, give us courage to... ." Then let the members pray in the blanks. Give them time; for some, this will be a new prayer experience. You could close this session by asking the group to join hands and read the "Verse for the Journey" in unison.

3 Recollecting and Reexperiencing

"Community Building"

You could open by reviewing the two previous healthy choices (the focus statements from the first two sessions) either by directly reading from page 11 and page 20 or by asking group members to restate the first two healthy choices in their own words. You can do this in Sessions 4, 5, and 6 as well. For the "Community Building" exercise, you could bring something you collect, noting that to collect is to gather or to bring together in one place. If the group is working well, you may decide to eliminate statements 2 and 3. Participants could be asked to bring in something they collect for this experience, although you will need to ask them to do so prior to the end of this session.

For the optional "Community Building," you will need to find some magazine pictures that will stimulate discussion. Paste or tape these pictures to posterboard or cardboard (they can be reused in future groups). After the community building, you might want to place the pictures where the group can see or refer to them during the session. Someone may have an "Aha!" moment after you have moved on; or you may want to do a picture review toward the end of the session to see if the discussion has stimulated further reflection on the picture.

"Discovery" sections

In response to Task 1, it did not take me long as a funeral director to learn that some widows and widowers do not have a deep pool of grief. Some are role-playing grief and they may feel enormously guilty about it. However, to verbalize the reality of their marriage or relationship would be quite threatening. If your group is largely composed of strangers, such admissions may be more likely. However, if the group members have known each other for a long time, you can expect some skating around this sensitive issue.

Let the group reflect on the Anne Sexton sidebar: "It doesn't matter who my father was; it matters who I remember he was." This will be tender turf for individuals who had unfinished business with the deceased or if there was a social stigma attached. For example, fathers of AIDS patients often grieve differently than mothers. Some participants may feel as if they are betraying confidences if a spouse does not—or more especially, will not—attend the group or share honestly with the group.

The family improvisation on Karen, Tim, and Meredith on page 36 can also be used in other sessions with just a little imagination. Expect the issue of quick remarriage to come up, particularly if there are "complications": the second spouse is much younger, or there is a suspicion that not enough is known about the person or the relationship had existed prior to a spouse's death. Finally, remember that the word "friend" these days has a wide meaning. Someone who is distraught over a "friend's" death could mean that the friendship had been intimate and/or sexual. Unresolved issues can create emotional discomfort for the group. The main goal of this session is summed up in the "Prayer for the Journey": "Give us the strength to be realistic, redemptive, and responsive in this season of grief."

"Wrap-up"

You may close with sentence prayers specifically for one of the three Rs: "Help me to be realistic (or redemptive or responsive) in this season of grief."

For the "Group Ministry Task," have members of the group write cards or notes to shut-ins or those who were part of the corporate prayers the previous Sunday.

If you are going to do a church-wide "Naming of Names" ritual (see pages 73-74), this would be a good time to review the plans and to finalize details. This group could assume responsibility for serving coffee and desserts afterwards. Gain commitments from the members. This is also a time for some members to be given names of individuals who should be contacted to see if they would like to participate in the "Naming of Names."

4 Relinquishing the Old Attachments

"Community Building"

Let the group reflect on the implications of the exercise on strength.

"Discovery" sections

In this session participants will confront the tendency to cling to the past and will be encouraged to relinquish old attachments.

In Task 1, "Inventory Your Attachments," you can set the tone by giving some direction on tangible and intangible attachments. Some participants—widows or widowers—will report they miss the "intimacy." Few will be specific enough to say sexual expression, although sexual expression may have been long absent due to the nature of the illness. Yet, this is a reality of loss. Some will feel guilty having sexual responses.

For some, the loss will be too recent for the griever to have made much "progress" in settling the estate or other matters.

"Wrap-up"

Ministry also includes reaching beyond the church. Adopt a community organization that serves people, such as a food shelf, clothing center, feeding program, homeless shelter, or AIDS-related organization. Organize a "pounding" (each person brings a pound or more of food). For example, if you are doing a "Naming of Names" service at the church, you could ask each person attending to bring an item of food. Members could also bring food items.

5 Readjusting to a New World

"Community Building"

The "Community Building" experience may be a challenge to some of your group; they may be good at giving compliments but find it difficult to receive compliments. You might want to put up newsprint around the room and as words are shared about a particular person, write these words under their names.

"Discovery" sections

When topics such as God's role in suffering and good and evil are discussed, people often have strong feelings or opinions. Some will want to argue and imply that their opinions only are correct. How can you respond? "Thank you for sharing your thoughts with us. I am wondering, though, if someone might have a differing opinion on this subject."

An additional option is to have members of the group read books on God's role in suffering and report back to the group.

"Wrap-up"

Make an appointment with a member of your pastoral staff to discuss making plans for a church Memorial Day tribute (any time of the year). This could be as simple as a reading of the names of those members of the church who have died in the last year. It could involve planning a display of pictures or a scrapbook. Ask about the option, in lieu of flowers at funerals, of contributions to the church library's grief collection. Then at the Memorial Day gathering, those resource additions to the library could be highlighted in the bulletin or by table display. Giving books in lieu of flowers is a way to help people feel that they have paid their respects.

6 Reaching Out to a New Future

"Community Building"

In the "Community Building" exercise, group size may determine how the exercise plays out. For a given category, for example, "Going to church alone," you could do a rapid discussion cruise around the group. This exercise could be used throughout the session, periodically stopping and drawing a topic, since the exercise ties in so well with the theme of this session.

Prepare an index card for the optional "Community Building" exercise. On one side write *Past Tense* and on the other, *Future Tense*. After the first go-around, they could pass the card again and ask, "What would it take to get me to future tense?"

"Discovery" sections

This session focuses on a delicate balance between active and passive grieving. Some grievers are take charge people. X has happened and this is how I respond. Some grievers rather enjoy the learned helplessness of grief, if they have enough supporters in their lives.

You could bring in a rearview mirror (from a junkyard or yard sale) and pass it around the group during the session as a visual prop.

As the discussion turns to Task 1 and its key question "Who am I without this significant person in my life?" you may want to use a chalkboard and chalk or newsprint and markers. Write each group member's name, and after reflection on the question, go around the group and ask each participant to call out two or three words or phrases that answer that question.

You can expect that some will have great difficulty with Anne Brener's words about transforming a relational loss from "a wound to a blessing."

"Wrap-up"

Many people, particularly senior adults, have a desire to visit the cemetery but are hesitant to go alone, either for physical or emotional security. Members of this group could be matched up with others in the church who wish to visit a loved one's grave. Simply, a note in the bulletin or an announcement of the group's availability for this service could be made.

This session would be a time to commit themselves to this important service to others. If your small group ended with the service, "The Naming of Names," perhaps a care center in your area would be open to your conducting a "Naming of Names" in their facility. Contact the care center and enlist volunteers for this opportunity to minister to others.

Expanding beyond six sessions

Expanding the six sessions for those who want to meet longer is possible in several ways.

- Because each theme is divided into three "Tasks," an eighteen-session format is possible by focusing each session on one "Task."

- There may certain topics or tasks that some group members would like to emphasize for an additional session focus. Some topics might be dealing with holidays and anniversaries, God and human suffering, and what the Bible teaches about death and grief.

- A person or two might be willing to read a book listed on page 78 and lead a session on it.

- Guests, such as a counselor, might be invited to join the group, perhaps to give a brief presentation with plenty of time to talk together.

- You may want to schedule a "Now that I have had time to think about this" session, perhaps thirty days after the completion of the last official session.

Using the resource as a retreat

This material can also be used in an intensive Friday to Sunday format or in a retreat format. A possible schedule would be to go through Session 1 on Friday night; Sessions 2, 3, and 4 on Saturday morning, afternoon and evening; and Sessions 5 and 6 on Sunday morning and early afternoon. A "Naming of Names" ceremony could be held as part of a worship service on Sunday morning.

Certainly, there are advantages and disadvantages to any format. Many participants like the fact that with weekly meetings, they have time to reflect on what they have learned. They get to know the group members better through six or more weeks of interaction.

On the other hand, a get-away weekend seminar offers a chance to be deliberately intense. Also, in a retreat setting, the participants are freed from daily obligations and responsibilities so that the clock will not determine how much the time they spend on the material. One additional benefit can be to use the intensive weekend experience to launch the study and then use the weekly sessions to build on that weekend.

The Naming of Names

The following guidelines will help you as you plan a "Naming of Names" service.

- One unlighted candle should be on the altar for each person being remembered in the service; this is why advance registration is required. As each name is read, the person(s) remembering that name should advance to the altar, take an unlighted candle and light it from the one burning candle, pause for a moment, then either kneel at the altar for a moment of personal reflection or return to their seat.

- At the close of the service, the candles are extinguished and given to the participants. You may wish to print the name of the remembered person on a white index card with a dark marker and slip the cards under the candles so that each participant can identify a particular candle.

- If the pastor wishes to participate, she or he could give a brief meditation; otherwise one could be given by a member of the group.

- If the "Naming of Names" is open to the congregation and non-participants join in the "Naming of Names," a brief time of reception afterwards would be appropriate.

- If the "Naming of Names" is part of the last session, you will need to plan this service as part of your time so that you will have less time to deal with the text than in previous weeks. Additionally, any wrap-up comments should be done before the ritual.

- It is desirable that this service be duplicated in an attractive format as a way of remembering the evening; prepare extras for sharing with family and friends. The outline that follows can be reworded so that it is suitable for a service bulletin.

Welcome

One or more persons read John 11:25-26, Job 19:25-27, and Romans 14:7-8.

All: Blessed are the dead who die in the Lord.

Leader: The Lord be with you.

All: And also with you.

Leader: Let us pray. You have blessed us, O God, with the gift of human love. We thank you for those who have blessed our lives and who we now pause to remember especially (names). We remember those who have loved us and those whom we have loved. We remember those who have shared our sorrows who have listened to our stories who have participated in our celebrations who have wept with us in our woundedness who have been there when we needed them.

This night (or day), O God of grace and glory, as we remember their lives and their witness give us faith to see in death the gate of eternal life so that, in quiet assurance, and with great hope, we may continue our course on earth, until, by your call, we are reunited with those we love, where there is no more death or sorrow or parting or crying. Amen.

Shared reading: Psalm 23

Leader: [Reads the first half of each verse]

All: [Read the second half]

Gospel: John 14:1-7

A sermon or reflection, if desired, may follow the reading of the Gospel.

Hymn

A hymn such as "For All the Saints" (*Lutheran Book of Worship*, 174) can be sung by a soloist or by the group; or it can be read in unison.

Intercessions

Leader: For all our loved ones who have died, let us pray to the God who said, "I am the resurrection and the life." We pray to God.

All: Hear us, O God.

Leader: God, you consoled Mary and Martha in their distress; draw near to us who in this place remember those who have died. We pray to God.

All: Hear us, O God.

Leader: God, you wept publicly at the grave of Lazarus, comfort us in our loss. We pray to God.

All: Hear us, O God.

Leader: God, you raised the dead to life; give to those we love who have finished their course in faith joyous eternal life. We pray to God.

All: Hear us, O God.

Leader: God, your days are without end and your mercy is without measure; make us aware of the shortness and uncertainty of human life, and let your Holy Spirit lead us in holiness and righteousness all the days of our life, so that, when we shall have served you in our generation, we too may be gathered to our ancestors and into your presence. We pray to God.

All: Hear us, O God.

The Calling of the Names

Leader: As the name of your loved one is read, you are invited to come forward and light a candle as a sign of your hope. You may kneel at the altar for a moment of private prayer and reflection or you may return to your seat.

(In the service bulletin, the name to be read appears in the left column and the name of the person remembering appears in the right column: for example, "David Alan Morrison remembered by Elizabeth Morrison.")

Closing prayer

Leader: God of all, we pray to you for those we know and love, but can no longer see. Grant them rest eternal and let light perpetual shine upon them. Grant your servants, whose memory we have celebrated, and to us that inheritance promised to all your saints. We ask this through Christ Jesus, to whom be glory forever and ever.

All: Amen.

The Blessing

All: May their memory to us be a blessing.

Appendix

Record information about group members here.

Names   **Addresses**   **Phone Numbers**

_____

_____

_____

_____

_____

_____

_____

_____

_____

_____

_____

"Do not be conformed to this world, but be transformed by the renewing of your minds, so that you may discern what is the will of God—what is good and acceptable and perfect" (Romans 12:2).

■ For our time together, we have made the following commitments to each other

■ Goals for our study of this topic are

■ Our group ministry task is

■ My personal action plan is

Prayer requests

_____

_____

_____

_____

_____

_____

_____

Prayers

■ Closing Prayer

Lord God, you have called your servants
to ventures of which we cannot see the
ending, by paths as yet untrodden,
through perils unknown. Give us faith to
go out with good courage, not knowing
where we go, but only that your hand is
leading us and your love supporting us;
through Jesus Christ our Lord. Amen.

Lutheran Book of Worship, copyright 1978, page 153

■ The Lord's Prayer

(If you plan to use the Lord's Prayer, record the version your group uses in the next column.)

Ambrose, Stephen E. *Eisenhower: Soldier and President,* New York: Simon and Schuster, 1990.

Barbo, Beverly. *The Walking Wounded.* Lindsborg, Kan.: Carlson's Publishers, 1987.

Boller, Paul F. *Presidential Wives.* New York: Oxford University Press, 1988.

Brener, Anne. *Mourning and Mitzvah.* Woodstock, Vt.: Jewish Lights, 1993.

Brownlee, Shannon. "The Narrowing of Normality." *U.S. News & World Report*, 22 August 1994.

Bush, Barbara. *Barbara Bush: A Memoir.* New York: Charles Scribner's, 1994.

Corr, Charles A. "Coping With Dying: Lessons That We Should and Should Not Learn From The Work Of Elisabeth Kubler-Ross," *Death Studies*, 17 (1993).

Lutheran Book of Worship. Minneapolis, Augsburg, 1978.

David, Lester and Irene David. *Ike and Mamie: The Story of a General and His Lady.* New York: G.P. Putnams, 1991.

Dean, Amy. *Proud to Be.* New York: Bantam, 1994.

Editors of Life. *Remembering Jackie: A Life in Pictures.* New York: Time/Warner, 1994.

Evans, Noela N. *Meditations for the Passages and Celebrations of Life.* New York: Bell Tower, 1994.

Fawzy, Fawzy I., Nancy W. Fawzy, and Robert O. Pasnau. "Bereavement in AIDS." *Psychiatric Medicine*, 9:3 (1991).

Kavanaugh, Robert. *Facing Death.* Los Angeles: Nash, 1972.

Koop, C. Everett. Koop: *The Memoirs of America's Family Doctor,* New York: Random House, 1991.

Lewis, C.S. *A Grief Observed.* New York: Bantam, 1961.

Lindemann, Erich. "Symptomatology and Management of Acute Grief." *The American Journal of Psychiatry*, 101 (1944): 141-148.

Morris, Edward. *The Rise of Theodore Roosevelt.* New York: Coward, McCann, and Geoghegan, 1979.

Pietsch, William V. *The Serenity Prayer Book.* San Francisco: HarperSanFrancisco, 1990.

Rando, Therese A. "The Increasing Prevalence of Complicated Mourning: The Onslaught Is Just Beginning." *Omega*, 26:1 (1993).

"Remembering Jackie," *Town and Country*, July 1994.

Simundson, Daniel J. *Where Is God In My Suffering?* Minneapolis: Augsburg, 1983.

St. Yves, Susanne. "Lights in the Darkness," *Sojourners*, June 1994.

Please tell us about your experience with INTERSECTIONS.

4. What I like best about my INTERSECTIONS experience is

5. Three things I want to see the same in future INTERSECTIONS books are

6. Three things I might change in future INTERSECTIONS books are

7. Topics I would like developed for new INTERSECTIONS books are

8. Our group had _____ sessions for the six chapters of this book.

9. Other comments I have about INTERSECTIONS are

_____

Thank you for taking the time to fill out and return this questionnaire.

- - - - - - - - - - - - - - - FOLD CARD IN HERE, SEAL WITH TAPE, AND MAIL TODAY! -

Please check the INTERSECTIONS book you are evaluating.

- ☐ Following Jesus
- ☐ The Bible and Life
- ☐ Captive and Free
- ☐ Caring and Community

- ☐ Death and Grief
- ☐ Divorce
- ☐ Faith
- ☐ Jesus: Divine and Human

- ☐ Men and Women
- ☐ Peace
- ☐ Praying
- ☐ Self-Esteem

Please tell us about your small group.

1. Our group had an average attendance of _____.

2. Our group was made up of
   _____ Young adults (19-25 years)
   _____ Adults (most between 25-45 years)
   _____ Adults (most between 45-60 years)
   _____ Adults (most between 60-75 years)
   _____ Adults (most 75 and over)
   _____ Adults (wide mix of ages)
   _____ Men (number) and _____ women (number)

3. Our group (answer as many as apply)
   _____ came together for the sole purpose of studying this INTERSECTIONS book.
   _____ has decided to study another INTERSECTIONS book.
   _____ is an ongoing Sunday school group.
   _____ met at a time other than Sunday morning.
   _____ had only one facilitator for this study.

BUSINESS REPLY MAIL
FIRST CLASS MAIL   PERMIT NO. 22120   MINNEAPOLIS, MN

POSTAGE WILL BE PAID BY ADDRESSEE

Augsburg Fortress
ATTN INTERSECTIONS TEAM
PO BOX 1209
MINNEAPOLIS MN 55440-8807

CPSIA information can be obtained
at www.ICGtesting.com
Printed in the USA
BVOW08s1550080218
507566BV00007B/90/P